Wallsend
Remembered
Volume Two

Another look back at growing up in
Wallsend, Howdon and Willington Quay

No. 111   High Street & Town Hall, Wallsend.

by Steve Boundey

'This book is dedicated to my wife, Audrey, and sons Daniel and Jack. Thanks once again for your patience and help'.

Previous page: The photograph on page one is taken from Wallsend Local History Society's archives and shows the Town Hall shortly after it was built. The foundation stone for the building was laid on 19th June 1907 by Mr William Boyd, the first Mayor of Wallsend and the building was opened by Alderman George A. Allan, the chairman of the Building Committee, on 16th September 1908. The foundation stone can still be seen, although a bit weathered and worn now, on the bottom of the left hand door pillar as you enter the Town Hall. The public clock was first started immediately after the opening ceremony by Miss Sylvia Stephenson, daughter of the then Mayor, Mr Christopher Stephenson.

Copyright Steve Boundey 2014

First published in 2014

Summerhill Books
PO Box 1210
Newcastle-upon-Tyne
NE99 4AH

www.summerhillbooks.co.uk

email: summerhillbooks@yahoo.co.uk

ISBN: 978-1-906721-82-4

Contents

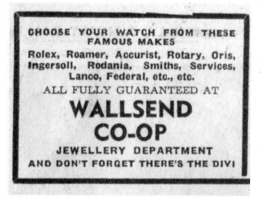

Two adverts for local shops taken from a 1958 copy of the Wallsend News.

Wallsend Local History Society

The Society meets in St Luke's Church Hall, Frank Street, Wallsend. Meetings are held on the 2nd Monday of each month at 7 pm to 9 pm.

As well as our well attended monthly meetings, we support a wide variety of local interests such as the Wallsend Festival where our stall arouses great interest with a display of old photographs of Wallsend. Our members also enjoy frequent bus outings.

To find out more about the Society, come along, you'll receive a warm welcome in a friendly atmosphere. Full membership is £8 per year. This fee covers everything except outings. Visitors, who are most welcome, are charged £2 for the evening.

Please visit our website at – www.wallsendhistory.btik.com

There are facilities for disabled persons.

Telephone: WALLSEND 623593   0445

Raymond Swan Ltd

THE FIRM FOUNDED ON FRIENDSHIP
94, HIGH STREET EAST, WALLSEND
VAT Reg. No. 176 1180 68   RADIO – TELEVISION

Mr Boundey.   15.11.1986.

17 Holderness Road
Howdon
Wallsend.

Panasonic TX2112
21" Colour Teletext T.V
TEAK.   £437.00

By deposit of.   200.00
                                  £237.00

£47.00 month over 4 months.
£49.00 last month.

ACCOUNT No.	AMOUNT PAID	BALANCE
445C	£37.00	£ FINAL.
SIG. ØM.	DATE 14/2/87	NAME BOUNDY

AUTOMATICKET LTD.   RAYMOND SWAN LTD.
A80408   94, HIGH ST. EAST, WALLSEND-ON-TYNE
                   *PHONE: 623593

Pictured are a Customer Payment Card from Grattan's, a receipt from Raymond Swan's TV Shop and a Terms of Tenancy from the 14 Storey flats.

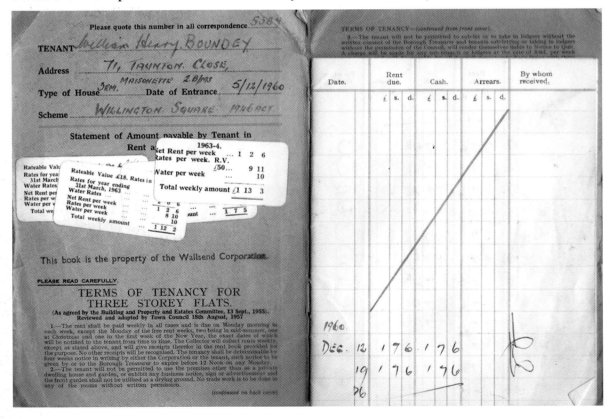

Introduction

I have once again been talking to lots of people I know following the last book I wrote, 'Wallsend Remembered.' Many of them have asked if there was going to be a second book but until I had enough material I could not say. Now, thanks to these people, strangers at first but becoming good friends with a love of local history and other friends, I have been able to put together this book and hope anyone reading will enjoy it. It is their memories I am trying to capture.

As mentioned in my last book, I grew up mainly living in Howdon, first in Taunton Close, one of the 14 Storey flats or '14ers' at Willington Square, by the Coast Road, before moving to High Howdon and the three storey flats at Windsor Drive and then Holderness Road in Howdon.

I still have fond memories of playing football and cricket and many other games on the 'big field'. This was a large field on Windsor Drive opposite the Wallsend Labour Club and next to the three storey flats. Now it is a housing development made up of Council houses.

On a Saturday with both my parents, Bill and Elsie Boundey, working all day my brother Billy and I used to go to my maternal grandparents to be looked after. They lived in Charlotte Street which runs north at a right angle to the front of the Town Hall. I was born at the Green Maternity Hospital and we used to play on the grassed area of this and the Hall Grounds, as well as down the Burn, where I remember we had a camp on the north bank of the Burn and used to have a brick construction as our main wall. Unbeknown to us this stone wall was once part of the structure of the old Waggon Way Bridge which used to cross the Burn. We used to play innocently by the Burn, but we did notice some of the old men playing 'Pitch and Toss', a sort of betting game where anyone unfortunate enough could lose a week's wages on the toss of a coin!

Again I have managed to obtain many old photographs and articles of schools, the local area, work places and teams. I have also included some lovely photographs of some of the older, more well-known buildings of Wallsend, some sadly gone forever.

In this book I have included some local people who became celebrities, big or small in some way and have dedicated a lot of space to my family's hero, my Dad. I have included many of his awards as he worked his way through the Boys' Brigade and the Royal Air Force to his becoming a well-respected motor mechanic and a special person in the lives of all who knew him. He married my Mam, his childhood sweetheart and I have told some of her story as she was growing up and facing evacuation. Our family is so proud of these two very special people.

This book is not meant to be a factual history of Wallsend – it is taken from people's memories, as they remember growing up and there may be some factual errors so an apology is made now for any mistakes.

I hope you will enjoy reading this book and hope it brings back some more good memories.

Steve Boundey
Wallsend, 2014

The Howdon Library Sculpture showing the history of the area.

Wallsend Remembered

The picture right is an artist's impression of how the Roman Fort of Segedunum is thought to have looked. You can see the horse and cart heading towards one of the gateways leading to the fort.

Hadrian's Wall originally started from Newcastle upon Tyne, which was known as 'Pons Aelius', and stretched west across the country to Chesters Roman Fort, 'Cilurnum'. It was later extended eastwards to a new fort at Wallsend, which was known as 'Segeduno' in the early fifth century. It was of Celtic origin and derived from the words 'sego' meaning 'strength' and 'dunum' meaning 'fortified place' with the name 'Segedunum' being translated as 'the Strong Fort'.

The modern name of 'Wallesende' was first recorded around AD 1085 and it was later changed to 'Wallsend'.

Recently it has been said that the wall did not indeed end at Wallsend but stretched eastwards to Tynemouth but it is my opinion that Wallsend is exactly as it describes – 'the end of the wall'.

The photograph above left shows a fragment of the Roman Wall found in the grounds of Wallsend Shipyard in 1903. The south east corner of the Camp is immediately in front of the house, which was called Camp House. The photograph was taken by Mr W.S. Corder. The photograph above right again shows Camp House but at a later date and at the time of this photograph more houses have been built to the left of the house. There was a stone built into the Camp House and was rescued when the house was demolished. It is now located in Segedunum Roman Fort.

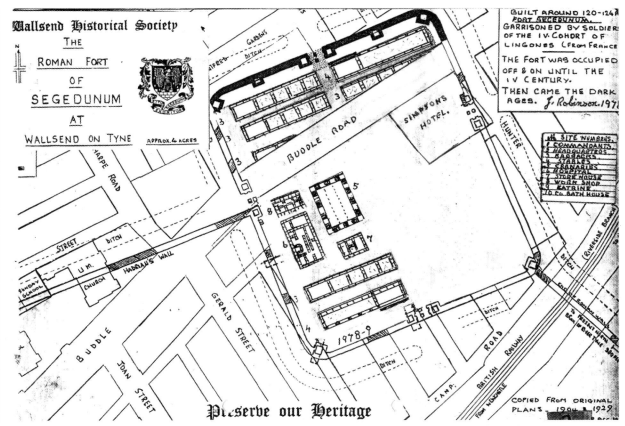

THE

ROMAN FORT

OF

SEGEDUNUM

AT

WALLSEND ON TYNE   APPROX. 4 ACRES

BUILT AROUND 120-124 A
FORT SEGEDUNUM.
GARRISONED BY SOLDIER:
OF THE IV COHORT OF
LINGONES (FROM FRANCE

THE FORT WAS OCCUPIED
OFF & ON UNTIL THE
IV CENTURY.
THEN CAME THE DARK
AGES. J. Robinson. 197

SITE NUMBERS.
1 COMMANDANTS.
2 HEADQUARTERS.
3 BARRACKS.
4 STABLES.
5 GRANARIES.
6 HOSPITAL.
7 STORE HOUSE.
8 WORK SHOP.
9 LATRINE.
10 C. BATH HOUSE.

Preserve our Heritage

COPIED FROM ORIGINAL
PLANS. 1904 & 1929

Above: A map drawn in 1978 showing the location of the Roman Fort of Segedunum.

Right and below: Two photographs of an area to the west of Segedunum Roman Fort, Stewart Terrace and the rear of Westfield and Neptune Bank.

The flats of Walker just to the west of The Avenue, which is classed as the border of Wallsend and Newcastle, can be seen in the photograph right.

A few of the vehicles seen in the photograph left are thought to be, left to right a Morris van, a Commer van, a Ford Popular van, a Wolseley or Morris car and a Ford car.

The photograph on the right is a mural which is painted on the side of a brick structure that houses a sub-station. Paid for by British Gas, it was painted by local artist Doug Ewan and unveiled in 1988 by the then mayor of Wallsend, Norman Hunter. It is located on Buddle Street opposite the entrance to Segedunum Roman Fort and Museum.

Walking through Wallsend and starting at the west end of High Street West during the 1960s the following pictures show the buildings you would have seen. On the south side of the high street used to stand the original Police Station (in the centre of the photo left), which is now an old folk's home.

On the other side of the street opposite the Police Station still stands the Duke of York public house. The photo below left shows the pub with the advertising boards for Sale Rooms looking east along the High Street. The photograph below right shows the pub with what looks like the number 20 bus heading down the High Street.

The old Police Station was replaced by the newer station (see page 13) in 1907. The Police Houses were added in 1927. A new state of the art Police Station has been built by the Silverlink Shopping Centre which now means the second police station has closed and may be demolished in the near future.

High Street West
R.B. Bryson and C.A. Lawrence

The following collection of photographs of High Street West and C.A. Lawrence's bakers shop were given to me at the launch of my book 'Wallsend Shops – Past and Present'.

The photo top left shows the tunnel, next to R.B. Bryson's, leading to what used to be 2H Taxis, a garage behind the High Street where my father used to work as a motor mechanic. Opposite R.B. Bryson's, across the High Street, was C.A. Lawrence's, a local bakers and confectioners shop.

The lady who gave me the photographs can be seen in the bottom right photograph and used to work in Lawrence's.

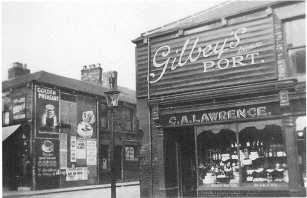

C.A. Lawrence's shop was located on the north side of High Street West just west of where the Ritz Bingo Hall stands now. Next door to this shop in later years was a motor shop, selling items for cars such as Duckham's motor oil etc.

The photograph above shows High Street West on what looks like a nice sunny afternoon. The Anchor Hotel can be seen on the south side of the street. It is still open today but is now called Last Orders. What does stand out to me is the lack of motor vehicles and road markings.

This photograph shows the shop of C.A. Lawrence proudly advertising 'The Champion of Bread Baking – 1921'. The advert on the wall to the left of the shop shows 'Winner of £300 National Trophy, London, September 7th 1921 – winner of the Silver Cup, Newcastle Exhibition 1911.' The cup is displayed in the window to the left of the door.

Wallsend High Street West showing the Forum and the Ship Hotel (now demolished). The Ship Hotel was the pub with the clock on the wall which can just be seen in the photograph.

Woolworths

The original Woolworths store used to stand approximately opposite the Ship Hotel on the north side of High Street West. In the 1950s the store moved to the site that most people remember, on the corner of Station Road and High Street East and is now Herons Foods. Can anyone remember the map which stood against the wall to the left of the front doors, roughly below where the sign is seen on the wall, behind the traffic signals in the photo? I can remember playing on this map; where you used to press the buttons to find a place and the lights would come on to show you where it was, when the lights worked!

Frank Woolworth opened his first store in Pennsylvania on 21st June 1879. It was unique at the time because it actually displayed the price of the items. The idea quickly caught on and similar stores opened across the United States and Canada before they were brought together in 1912 as a chain called F.W. Woolworths Company.

Wallsend's 'Woollies' started at 73-75 High Street West in 1930 and moved to the corner site in 1958. The store closed on 3rd January 2009.

Elton Street West, looking east towards Station Road, before the Forum was built. The four photographs below show the same area in Wallsend, the corner of Station Road and High Street West, behind where Martin's Bank used to stand.

On the right are the police houses and part of the station which stands on Alexander Street next to the recently closed Wallsend Library. Built in 1907, the date stone can be seen above the main entrance of this police station, facing the Library (photo below left.

Below right is the newest police station on Middle Engine Lane.

The photo on the right shows the inside of one of the cells in the Police Station on Alexander Road. The photo above shows the door to cell number 3.

Wallsend Slipway

Wallsend Slipway and Engineering Company came into existence on 18th November, 1871. It was built to provide a slipway for the repair of ships belonging to three large firms, Messrs C. Mitchell & Co of Walker, Messrs Watts Milburn & Co of Blyth and Newcastle and Messrs Nelson, Donkin & Co of North Shields. The Tyne Improvement Commission put down river training walls and the site for Wallsend Slipway was located between these walls and a high water mark near Point Pleasant.

A Tynemouth contractor, William Jackson, laid down two slipways, each measuring 1,000 metres.

At first the company acted solely as a slipway until 1874 when Mr William Boyd became managing director. He was more interested in engines than in shipbuilding and in 1878, after the first steel boiler was built on the Tyne, the word Engineering was added to the company name.

A dry dock was opened in 1895 and in 1905 the manufacture of steam turbines began, including those for the 'Mauretania'.

Above is a share certificate from the company dated 1906 and below is a cheque for £115, 5 shillings and 6 pence – a huge amount of money then, dated 10th June 1885.

The above information comes from the book 'History of the Parish of Wallsend' by William Richardson which was first published in 1923. Pictures from Wallsend Local History Society.

Places We Lived
Wallsend

Gordon Square, seen on the right, used to be located on Elton Street, near to where the Forum car park now stands.

The blocks of buildings were quite intimidating to many people.

The two pictures below show an area to the north of High Street West – Wanless Street.

The photograph on the left shows Shiney Row, on what is now North Street West. Behind the houses can be seen the tower of the Buddle School, which stands on Station Road.

Willington Quay

These photographs show the houses that were known as Keelman's Row. They had been in existence from around 1841 at least. They were built for the people who used to work on the keel's (broad, flush decked barges carrying cargo) on the River Tyne and in the census of 1841 it was noted that almost all of the heads of the households were in fact keelmen.

The keelmen were especially known for carrying coals from the spouts along the river to waiting collier brigs. Steam tugs gradually began to replace them however.

In 1861 none of the occupants were described as keelmen although there were three 'watermen'.

In later years the houses were completely taken over by shipyard workers. They used to stand in the shadow of the Willington Viaduct, at the bottom of Millers Bank, to the west of the Railway public house, now the Bogie Chain, seen on the right hand side of the bottom photograph, and the Dun Cow public house and Haggie's Ropeworks, both to the south.

The above photo has been dated to around some time after summer of 1930, due to the absence of wires over the tramlines. Wallsend Council began demolishing the houses in March 1932 so the bottom photograph is from that year.

The photograph on the right shows Norman Terrace looking east towards Percy Main. The church on the left was the Primitive Methodist Chapel.

The foundation stone for the church was laid in August 1880 and it opened at Easter in 1881. The public house in the far distance is the Shipwrights' Arms and the whole location is approximately where the Tyne Vehicular Tunnel is now situated. Part of Norman Terrace still exists today.

The photographs below show Palmer's Terrace, Willington Quay. One of the earliest references to this street's existence was in the 1894 survey and it is thought that Palmer's Terrace had presumably taken its name from the nearby shipyard of Charles Palmer.

The Palmer's Willington Quay yard closed in 1912. The area was thought to have been scheduled for demolition before the Second World War but the last occupants – possibly Crozier, Malia, Wallis, Taylor and Lough – were listed in the electoral roll of October 1956. The street was closed in February 1963 to allow Commercial Plastics to extend their premises. (Information taken from an old copy of the 'Wallsend News'.)

Potter Street, Willington Quay. This picture was supplied by Michael Doolan and shows the Pearl Cinema on the left. The photo below shows the staff of the Pearl with children queuing up to go in and was thought to be taken on the opening day, 21st November 1910.

Potter Street, Willington Quay. 3758

The photo on the left is of a young boy standing with his bike in front of one of Willington Quay landmarks – the Ballast Hill, used for loading the ships on the River Tyne.

This photograph shows a local shop on Potter Street in Willington Quay. The large wall on the left is part of the Turk's Head Hotel. Photograph supplied by Malcolm Dunn.

Low Willington Villa – This large house once stood on Ropery Lane, by Keelman's Row, and was once owned by the Hood Haggie family. The villa is mentioned in William Richardson's 'History of the Parish of Wallsend' and he recalls that 'Mr Stevenson Haggie married Miss Kate Stewart in May 1884 and they began their married life in the Villa. They moved out in June 1904 with Mr and Mrs Frank Dean becoming the new occupiers. In 1912, when the Deans moved to Jesmond, the Villa and grounds were attached to spacious dining-rooms built for the Ropery workers.'

Howdon and Rosehill

The above photograph, supplied by Malcolm Dunn, shows Willington Square around 1933 with the Coast Road in the foreground and Edward Pit to the right.

In an old issue of the Wallsend News, dated Friday, 3rd January 1953, the following extract was found about the area known as Willington Square.

In a story from the 'Down Your Street' series:

If we could make one New Year wish, it would be that each of our Down Your Street series would be as easy and as pleasant to write as has been Embleton Avenue and Gibson Street.

In these two streets which cross the Coast Road forming the shape of an arrow-head we have found no-one who had any spectacular claims to fame, but a friendly welcome and helpful advice from the miners and their wives and families was given to us at every door.

Here live people who have spent almost a lifetime winning coal, whose entire working lives have been spent in the dark, wet, underground seams robbing the earth of one of its most precious minerals in one of the hardest jobs in the world. And so it is perhaps appropriate that we begin the New Year with the tale of two streets which have seen so many New Years.

First to Embleton Avenue, a row of low houses which begins at the side of the Coast Road and then plunges off northwards towards the open fields. As we stand at the beginning of the row we can see the pit heap and the Rising Sun winding gear in the distance.

Mr and Mrs John Donnison, of 1 Embleton Avenue, moved into their house three months before the 1926 strike began. Since those grim days they have lived there and, happily, have seen better times.

Aged 66, Mr Donnison began work at the 'G' Pit as a 13 year-old trap boy, opening and closing trap doors. Then he went to the Rising Sun pit and worked through all of the underground trades.

In 1942 he left the pit and went to work at Wallsend Slipway as a plater's helper. He worked there until 1951.

Mr Donnison was born in Walker and moved to Wallsend 50 years ago. He lived for a time in Jubilee Street. His wife Sarah, aged 60, was bred and born in Rosehill. They have a family of three, two sons and a daughter.

When we called at number 3 Embleton Avenue we found only Mrs Maria Parker at home. Her husband, Herbert, a deputy at the Rising Sun, was at the pit. Mr Parker, we learn, has been working at the Rising Sun for 22 years. They have a family of four sons and a daughter. Their eldest son, William, is an electrician at the Rising Sun.

'Try anything once' has been the motto of Mr George Toward of number 17 Embleton Avenue, and it is a motto which he has carried out to the letter. When he retired from the Rising Sun in 1952, at the age of 73 where he had been a deputy, Mr Toward had a very full life to look back on.

During the two World Wars he served as an ARP Warden, a special constable and a member of the St John Ambulance Brigade. He still has certificates, given to him at the time of his joining these voluntary bodies, which he showed us. They are indeed very impressive, and soon his table was littered with certificates. There was one for his work as a fire warden, another for his special constable duty, signed by the Prime Minister of the time – Baldwin, and a certificate acknowledging his work as a Red Cross and St John Ambulance worker during the Second World War. And we also found one for services rendered in the Tynemouth Ambulance Corps. 'I gave everything a go' he told us.

He has been a 'Buff' since 1919, and was a trainer to the old Preston Colliery Football Club (now North Shields AFC) for some time.

He moved to Preston Colliery where he worked for 33 years. When only a boy and working in the mines he had both legs, an arm and seven ribs broken in an accident. He later became a deputy and chargeman at Preston and Wallsend Collieries. He has some old pay notes which date from the time at Wallsend and Hebburn Coal Co, and they make interesting reading. For a seven-shift week in those days he was paid £2.6s.3d. For working a wet shift he was paid 4d extra.

Across from Mr Toward's house are four houses standing on their own, they are pebbled and the exposed brick is clean and new-looking. These four houses have an interesting history and who better to tell us than 87 year-old Mr Thomas Dent, the Grand Old Man of these two streets, and possibly Willington Square too.

Mr Dent started work when he was 12. He was a 'coupling-on' boy. 'We used to couple the tubs

Embleton Avenue.

together,' he said, smiling as he recalled those far-away days. He came to Wallsend when he worked at the 'G' Pit and then the Rising Sun. He retired at the age of 70.

His house, in which he has lived for 18 years, was once an officials' institute. Later it was opened as a miners' club and Mr Dent recalled the happy hours he spent when it was a club. Mrs Dent, aged 85, was born in Wallsend. They had a family of eight. Now there are three boys and a girl living.

At number 21 Embleton Avenue lives Mr Gordon Askew, aged 72, who still works at the Rising Sun stores, and his wife Ann, aged 65. They have lived here for 25 years and both are Wallsend-born. Parents of two sons and two daughters, they are keen members of Hadrian Road Methodist Church, and Mr Askew and his eldest son are well-known Methodist preachers. Mrs Askew was christened at the church and has attended all her life. Her husband has been attending for about 50 years.

Crossing the Coast Road and going to Gibson Street let us knock upon number 15. Here live Mr and Mrs Joseph Smith. Mr Smith, aged 66, worked at the Rising Sun pit for 52 years and is now working at the old 'G' Pit on the winder. He started work at the old Edward Pit until it closed in 1930. Although his father was not a miner, he was born in the pit cottages at Willington Road Row and as a boy ran errands for the miners. Mr and Mrs Smith have two daughters, both of whom are married.

Mr Dan (Danny) Vale, lives at number 18 Gibson Street. He and his wife Deborah, both aged 53. Mr Vale works at the pit and they have lived in Gibson Street for 22 years. Mrs Vale lived in the house before she was married. They have one daughter, married who lives in Derwent Gardens; 'nice and handy' says Mrs Vale.

Almost any fine day you can see a little old lady tending her garden in Gibson Street. She is widowed Mrs Edith Robson, aged 70, of number 30. She has two daughters and three sons. Her eldest son is a joiner and lives with her. Her husband was a filler at the Rising Sun. She has lived here for 35 years during which time her garden has given her increasing pleasure. 'I always like to keep busy.' To all the children around she is known as 'Gannie Robson' and though they all run when she catches them in her garden, they often call in to show her new toys or to air a grievance.

One of the first people to come into Gibson Street after it was built lives at number 43. She is Mrs Catherine Cain, a 70 year-old widow who lives there with her two sons and married daughter. 'When we first moved in, the street was called Dene View,' said Mrs Cain. 'It was changed to Gibson Street years later.' She also recalled the waggon-way which was built through the street to haul away the clay which was being dug up.

'There was no lighting or pavement,' she added. 'We had to walk all the way down to Wallsend over the Dene.' Her husband was a miner at the Edward Pit, and they have a family of six sons and two daughters. Five of her sons are miners.

There are about 1,300 miners working at the Rising Sun and Mr George Cook of number 49 Gibson Street sees all of them during his work as a time-keeper at the colliery. Aged 63, Mr Cook came to Wallsend in 1921, and lived in a house at the top of Gibson Street until the Coast Road was built. Then it was found necessary to demolish his house so they moved down to number 49. He came to Wallsend to work at the old Edward Pit until it closed in 1930.

He also worked at the 'G' Pit as a weighman. After the Edward Pit closed he came to work at the Rising Sun as a time-keeper. It is his job to check in the entry and departure of the underground workers. Mr Cook, like so many others in the area, carries on a family tradition, for his father was employed in the mines before him. Mrs Cook, aged 62, was born in Sunderland, but came to Wallsend when five years-old. They have one son who works at the Rising Sun as a fitter.

Gibson Street.

At number 47 lives Mr and Mrs John Joseph Wood. Aged 75 and still working, Mr Wood has worked in all branches of mining – 'I've done the lot,' he says. Now a grey-haired wrinkled old gentleman, he tells us that he first began working as a boy of 14 in a pit in Cumberland. At the age of 17 he worked at a Walker Colliery and then in 1900 went down the 'G' Pit where he worked for ten years. Then he worked at the Rising Sun where he has worked since and where he is now one of the oldest men there. Mrs Wood, aged 72, was born in Wallsend and they have a family of five girls and three boys and 20 grand-children. 'Whenever I go out I hear someone shouting 'Granda' at me,' said Mr Wood.

At number 23 Gibson Street lives Mr Thomas Mitchinson, who lives with his daughter and her husband. Mr Mitchinson began work at a Cumberland mine and came to Wallsend in 1910 where he worked at the 'G' Pit for a while, then moved on to Walker and later to Backworth. Returning to Wallsend, he worked at the Edward Pit and was secretary of the local miners' lodge for seven years. Later he was transferred to the Rising Sun.

Stepping into the street, the houses are built together in pairs, with a space between each pair and they curve away from the Coast Road, to the open fields of the Dene, which once gave its name to the street.

The photos on this page are taken from my family album with the first one, Holme Gardens with the Bewicke First School in the background. The four children in the main group are back row, left to right – John and Nancy Boundey. Front row, left to right – Tommy and George Boundey.

The photo right shows part of the Boundey family, left to right – uncle George, grandfather Jack, uncle John, grandmother Martha and my dad, Bill.

On the far right, Doreen, wife of John, and George Boundey messing around on George's butchers bike, which he used when he worked for a local butcher in Howdon.

In this photo are Doreen Boundey, George Boundey and two of my cousins, sitting in the back garden of my grandparents' house in Hazelwood Terrace. On the left you can just see an old mangle which was used to squeeze the water out of newly washed clothes. How many people can remember these?

Buildings of Interest
Wallsend Memorial Hall

The Memorial Hall was built in 1883 by shipbuilder Sir G.B. Hunter. In 1925 an extension was added and the Hall was dedicated in honour of the employees of Swan, Hunter & Wigham Richardson Ltd who gave their lives in the First World War. A plaque was later added to the memorial to commemorate those men who died in the Second World War.

In April 2014 the Memorial Hall was the venue for a live broadcast of the BBC's Football Focus programme. The show was a celebration of Wallsend's football history – in particular the work over the years of the Boys' Club. Two former Boys' Club players – Alan Shearer and Alan Thompson appeared alongside Mark Lawrenson. There were also interviews from other Wallsend old boys – Michael Carrick of Manchester United and Hull City manager Steve Bruce.

The highlight of the programme for many was when a young lad from Wallsend Boys' Club asked Alan Shearer: 'For a million pounds would you wear a Sunderland shirt?'

After a long pause the former Newcastle United forward answered: 'Yes – if the money went to charity.'

Willington Mill

Haggies Ropeworks was located at Willington Quay and ran along the west side of the 'Gut' – a small tributary of the Tyne. The largest floor area was over a mile long and was known as the 'Long Pull' because they used the distance to measure the length of the ropes they were making.

The business was started up by Robert Hood Haggie, after a family argument which saw him leave the family firm in Gateshead and set up his own company in Willington Quay.

Robert Hood Haggie died in 1866 and his sons Robert, Stevenson and Arthur Jamison Haggie succeeded him.

A large part of the ropeworks was destroyed by a fire on 3rd June 1873. It was only due to the determined efforts of the local fire services and Railway Company that saved the Willington Viaduct, built between 1837-39, which ran overhead.

Haggies Ropeworks claimed the record for the longest continuous wire rope, of 14.9 miles, made for the Central Electricity Board, in 1983.

A glass window panel with the name: 'R. Hood Haggie & Son'.

A replica of a coil of rope, on the site of the former Haggies Ropeworks, that stands outside the front of what is now Bridon Ropes.

An old desk from the offices of Haggie's.

Wallsend Civic Hall

This photograph shows the Civic Hall when it was used as part of the hospital. Photo supplied by Denise Booth.

The Civic Hall was built in the 1800s, although there has been a building on this site since 1600s. It has been the residence of many great men of Wallsend's past including Sir George Hunter and Robert Richardson Dees.

Another lesser-known resident was William Clarke, who made the decision to renovate the original Holy Cross Church which overlooked the Burn. Having taken the roof off however, William Clarke decided to move away from Wallsend leaving the Church without its roof to eventually fall into ruin.

The following photos were taken on a September Heritage Open Day and show the kitchen on the left and circular ceiling window which is at the top of the main hallway and staircase.

The photos below show what was once the wine cellar and some older brickwork in the cellar which seem to lead intriguingly further down under the building.

There are rumours of underground tunnels which lead off between what used to be the stables of the Hall and the cellar. There are also tunnels said to be running from under the main entrance, southwards under the Village Green heading towards the River Tyne, under the junction of High Street and Station Road, under St Luke's Church (it is claimed there were cracks on the wall of the church, now repaired, which were due to subsidence due to the tunnels) and on to what used to be Carville Hall down by the river. The theory is that these tunnels were said to be escape routes for the owners of the Hall. Whether these stories are true or not, has yet to be proven.

The photo left shows what was once the entrance door to the Green Maternity Hospital. This is the place I was born in December 1960.

The building was first proposed to be used as a hospital in 1923 and it admitted its first patients on 3rd February 1925. Miss J.P. Keesey, was employed as Matron. The Wallsend and Willington Quay General Infirmary had its official grand opening in September 1925.

On 8th January 1949, an ex-glass cleaning station became the new maternity wing of the renamed Sir G.B. Hunter Memorial Hospital. The opening of the new wing was performed by the former chair of the hospital management committee, R.E. Smedley, and the Mayor and Mayoress of Tynemouth, Councillor and Mrs W.R. Forster and the Mayor and Mayoress of Wallsend, Alderman and Mrs P.J. McArdle were also present. The listed building closed to in-patient services by 1994 and was used as an Elderly Resource Centre from 1996. (Information from a copy of the 'Wallsend News'.)

The photograph right shows the Civic Hall as it is today, now Wallsend Hall including a cafe, and in the background is part of the old sun-ray hospital.

Wallsend Town Hall

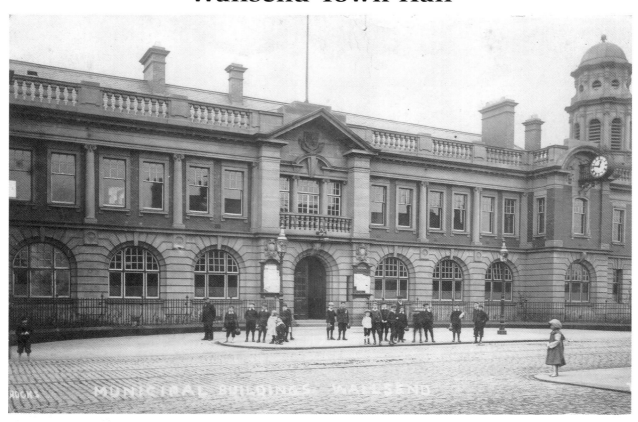

During the 1880s Wallsend's councillors used a number of flats in Elton Street for their meetings and from 1891 the Guardians' Hall was pressed into service. From 1901 the meetings were held in the Masonic Lodge. Land was bought in 1900 but it was not until 1905 when designs were submitted and accepted by Liddle & Brown of Newcastle for a new Town Hall.

The foundation stone (see bottom photo) was laid by ex-Mayor William Boyd on 19th June 1907. The opening ceremony was held on 16th September 1908 and was officiated by Alderman George A. Allen and Miss Stephenson, the Mayor's daughter, received a gold brooch and started a bracket clock built by Potts & Sons of Leeds, a gift from William Boyd.

The Municipal Buildings included the Town Hall, Police Courts, Fire Station and Swimming Baths.

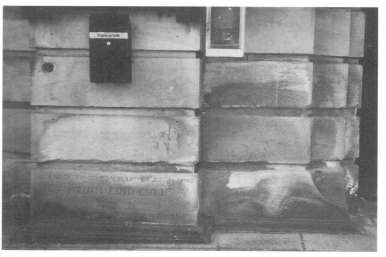

The photographs below are of the inside of the Town Hall with the Judge's chair from the Court Room and the Town Hall plaque and the Police Courts cells.

Masonic Lodge

In 1890 a proposal was made to move the First Lodge of the Freemasons to the Masonic Hall on Station Road. The foundation stone can be seen on the corner of the building, half-way up the wall. It was laid on Monday, 1st April, 1891 by Sir Matthew White Ridley, R.W. Prov. G.M. of Northumberland. The architect was Bro. Wm Hope of North Shields and it was built by a local builder, Bro. Wm Thos. Weir, of Howdon. The cost of the building was £2,500. Information from William Richardson's 'History of the Parish of Wallsend'.

More information can be found in George Laws' book – 'A History of Freemasonry in Wallsend'.

Local People
Mayor William Rickleton

Councillor William Rickleton was mayor of Wallsend from 23rd May 1960, taking over from Councillor J.G. Grogan, until he passed on the title of Mayor of Wallsend to Councillor J.H. Branch on 24th May 1961.

The photo right shows Mayor of Wallsend, Councillor W. Rickleton, with Town Clerk Mr J. Stoker walking past the Guard of Honour at St Peter's Church for the Mayor's Sunday Service in 1960/61. Burnside School, with the old entrance, can be seen in the background

Mayor Rickleton with Commanding Officer Major C.C. Reed, inspecting 506 Field Squadron, Royal Engineers (Territorial Army) before granting them Freedom of Borough, on the Green.

Mayor Rickleton presenting Major C.C. Reed of 506 Field Squadron Royal Engineers with the casket and scroll for the Freedom of the Borough. Looking on is Brigadier J.H. Carrera.

(Photos of Mayor Rickleton have been provided by his daughter, Christine.)

Mayor Elsie Halliburton

The photograph far right shows the retiring Mayor, Councillor W. Savory, presenting the robes to the new Mayor, Mrs E. Halliburton, with Town Clerk Mr John Stoker looking on.

The following is an extract taken from a local newspaper article, possibly the Evening Chronicle: 'Councillor Mrs Elsie Halliburton, of Edward Road, Rosehill, was chosen to be the next Mayor of Wallsend, taking over from Councillor W. Savory on 18th May 1970 to 15th May 1971, following a meeting at Wallsend Council. Her Mayoress will be her daughter, Mrs Elsie Booth of Kendal Gardens, High Howdon, who is on the staff of Dukes and Marcus Ltd, North Shields. Councillor Mrs Halliburton has been a member of the council since 1956, representing the Willington Quay ward for Labour. She acted as Mayoress seven years ago when Councillor Mrs E.M.A. Brown was Mayor of Wallsend. Councillor Mrs Halliburton's election was moved by Councillor J.P. Dixon and seconded by Alderman Mrs D. Sowerby and there were no other nominations.'

Help the old and lonely

In her inaugural speech, the new Mayor made an appeal to the people of Wallsend to do all they can to help the lonely and the elderly in the borough: 'There is a great need for everyone who can to do a little extra for the old people in the town,' Councillor Mrs Halliburton said. 'One of the greatest problems of the elderly is loneliness and there are a great many who are extremely lonely.'

Mayor of Wallsend, Councillor Elsie Halliburton and German guests from Rheydt, Wallsend's twin town, at the unveiling of the name plate at Rheydt Avenue, the approach road to Wallsend Sports Centre. At Rheydt in Germany, one of the thoroughfares is named Wallsend Promenade.

The Mayor of Wallsend sending down the first wood after opening the new bowls pavilion at Wallsend Sports Centre. Looking on are the Mayoress, Mrs Olive Lisgo, Councillor Mrs E.M. A. Brown, Mr John Todd, chairman of the former Wallsend Sports Club, who donated the pavilion and vice-chairman of Wallsend Sports Trust, officials and guests.

Olive shared the role of Mayoress with her sister Elsie.

The Freedom of Wallsend casket, holding the freedom scroll, being presented to Lieutenant L. McLeman by the Mayor of Wallsend at a colourful ceremony at The Green, Wallsend.

Councillor Mrs Elsie Halliburton, retiring, installing Councillor J.B. Wood as Mayor of Wallsend at Wallsend Town Hall. Looking on is the Town Clerk, Mr John Stoker.

Mrs Elsie Booth

Elsie Booth became the new Mayoress of Wallsend when her mother, Councillor Elsie Halliburton, became the Mayor. She was the wife of David Booth, Apprentice Training Supervisor at George Angus factory on the north side of the Coast Road, opposite the 14 Storey flats. (Neither the factory nor the flats have survived due to demolition.)

Mrs Halliburton had been a Wallsend Councillor since 1956 prior to becoming Mayor and had served as Mayoress in 1963. Elsie Booth was assisting her mother for only the first six months of her role as Mayor between 1970-71. Then Mrs Halliburton's older daughter, Mrs Olive Lisgo, was to take over as Mayoress for the remainder of the civic year.

Elsie Booth enjoyed her role as Mayoress and she is seen here along with her mother the Mayor, with a big smile on her face giving a civic send off to members of the Rising Sun Legionnaires Jazz Band, including Sandra Wilson, Shirley Sansom and Lynne O'Shaughnessy (apologies if the names are spelled incorrectly) before they left from outside the Town Hall on a sponsored walk around the borough boundary of Wallsend in aid of funds.

Sadly, Elsie died on 6th May 2012. The following information is taken from the Eulogy at Elsie's funeral:

Elsie Booth was born at No 2 Willington Stables, Wallsend in September 1933. She was the daughter of Robert and Elsie Halliburton and the third youngest of a family of eight. She lived in Edward Road, Rosehill throughout her childhood and remained in the locality for the remainder of her life.

Her first job was as an overlocker/machinist at Dukes and Markus Clothing Factory on Norham Road, North Shields. Elsie met her husband David (Davy) around 1953 at a dance at Wallsend Memorial Hall. They married three years later at St Mary's Church, Howdon on 16th September 1956 when she was 23.

Elsie and her sister, Anne were amazed to appear in a 'Presto' advert on ITV in the 1970s

In the 1970s Elsie was an avid supporter of 'The Revellers' Juvenile Jazz Band and was later heavily involved with the Willington Quay and Howdon Boys' Club where she was a chairperson for many years and received the Silver Award for 25 years Voluntary Service to Youth. Her husband Davy had received the Gold Award for 30 years service. After a lengthy time of illness, Elsie sadly passed away peacefully on 6th May 2012.

Doris Day's version of this song was played at Elsie's funeral, which summed up her life:

If I can help somebody as I pass along,
If I can cheer somebody with a word or a song,
If I can show somebody he is travelling wrong,
Then my living shall not be in vain.

David Booth

David Booth was a local lad who became a well known boxing champion. He lived in Percy Street, Wallsend, then Rothbury Gardens, Rosehill and was proud to represent Willington Quay and Howdon Boys' Club. David, or Davy, fought at cruiserweight, light-heavyweight and heavyweight levels. He was the wartime Imperial Services Light-Heavyweight Champion and became the International Services Champion in 1950 and the Royal Navy Champion in 1951.

Davy later had a spell of professional boxing but, even though he won his two fights, he preferred the atmosphere of amateur boxing and so retired to spend his time training young boxers at the Boys' Club.

A NEW NORTHERN STAR

DAVE BOOTH Wallsend

In later years he worked at George Angus' Factory on the north side of the Coast Road, earning great respect as the Apprentice Training Supervisor. He was awarded the British Empire Medal in the 1959 New Year's Honours list for his outstanding services. At the age of only 47, Davy had to take early retirement from George Angus Factory due to his deterioration caused by Motor Neurone Disease. Over 100 of his ex-Apprentices surprised him at the Blue Flames Sports Ground and awarded him with a fantastic model, which was made up of all the tools the apprentices used.

One of Davy's great loves and a place close to his heart was the Willington Quay and Howdon Boys' Club. The Boys' Club lost their premises when the British Legion was taken over for redevelopment (the old boys' club was by Mickey's in Rosehill) and Davy was determined to obtain the club some new premises.

His dream came true when the Duchess of Gloucester opened the new club on Archer Street on 7th October 1980 (see photograph above).

To mark his contribution to the club he served with throughout his life the Duchess rewarded Davy, the 49-year-old father of two, with the National Association of Boys' Clubs highest honour, a gold medal.

Above: The Duchess of Gloucester about to break off at the pool table in the new club on 7th October 1980.

Davy never forgot it was Willington Quay that put him in the boxing ring and the day the new club opened was 'the proudest day of his life', beating the receiving of the gold medal.

Sadly, Davy lost his final fight to Motor Neurone Disease and passed away just two days after the club opened.

Willington Quay and Howdon Boys' Club – This building now has a nice painting on the side of it. The sports hall had a plaque with 'The David Booth Hall' on which they added after Davy died.

Elspeth Landells Lammie, known as Elsie

My mother, Elspeth Landells Lammie, known as Elsie, was born on 8th December 1933 in Wallsend. She was one of five daughters of Hugh and Dorothy Lammie. Hugh was originally from the Isle of Skye who came to Wallsend looking for employment. He met a local lass, Dorothy High, and they fell in love and married and lived with their children in Charlotte Street, Wallsend.

Elsie and her sister, Patricia, known as Pat, were evacuated to a big house in the country near Wooler which belonged to Major and Mrs Briggs (affectionately known as Mammie).

Many thanks go to the Alnwick Local History Society who were contacted and recognised the house from the first photograph below and it is now known to be Thornington House. However, as the story has been passed on to me, although Pat loved the house and wanted to stay there, Elsie did not like being evacuated and taken away from her family and was much happier when they were re-united after the war.

Left are two photographs of Thornington House. The photo below left was taken on Whit Monday, 1971, when Pat paid a return visit with her daughters, Michelle, Dorothy and Jackie, to see Mrs Briggs, who sadly passed away on 6th January 1979. Photograph supplied by Michelle and Dorothy, Pat's daughters.

The photo at the top of the page is one of a number that are thought to be from a collection that were sent to my grandparents, Hugh and Dorothy at Charlotte Street to show that Elsie and Pat had settled in nicely with Major and Mrs Briggs and were enjoying their new life style in the country. Elsie is holding one of her favourite toys. They were probably made to be comfort toys which would hopefully help if and when they felt homesick. Personally, I would think being taken away from your family and not being able to see them or phone them up when you wanted to and living with people who you had never met before, would be a very daunting experience, not just for my mother and her sister, but for thousands of evacuated children all over the country.

I do not know why it was just two children out of five who were evacuated from my mam's family but there must have been a reason for it.

Elsie met my father, William Boundey when she was a young girl and they fell in love and married on 11th November 1954. Elsie had many jobs including working in Ruddick's fruit shop on the High Street, Presto's in the Forum, the VG in Howdon and

Sanderson's sweet shop on Tynemouth Road. She was very well liked and had a bubbly character. She suffered from ill health, including a battle against cancer, and she sadly passed away on the 3rd May 1979 at a far too young age of 45. She is still deeply missed by all of her family.

Right: Elsie, aged 7 and Pat, aged 5, in the garden of Thornington House. Although I did not know how big Thornington House was then, these days it seems to be a sprawling estate with woods and green pastures. I can only imagine what adventures my mam and auntie used to get up to. It would have been a world of difference from a terraced flat with outside toilets and washing hanging up in the back lanes with the smell of home baking in the air, in a town like Wallsend.

William Henry Boundey, known as Bill

My father, William Boundey, or Bill, was born on 11th November 1932. He lived most of his younger years in Howdon with his parents, at 35 Hazelwood Terrace, behind the Stephenson Memorial Middle School, and then moved to 2 Elizabeth Road.

Like most young boys in those days he joined the Boys' Brigade and was very proud of the badges he gained whilst in the Brigade. He attended the Stephenson Memorial School and after leaving he joined the Royal Air Force Air Training Corps, enlisting at Cardington and ended up at RAF Weeton, near Blackpool.

He used to make his way back to Wallsend whenever he could to meet his childhood sweetheart, Elsie Landells Lammie, often hitching a lift either all of the way to Newcastle or to the nearest train station.

Bill started working as an apprentice Motor Mechanic which was his trade throughout his life,

working at the garage on the Coast Road, before working at Denney's Motors, at the west end of Wallsend High Street, 2H Taxis at Portugal Place, Gordon Square Garage behind what is now the Forum, Wallsend Motor Company and ending his working days at Blue Line Taxis, Sycamore Street.

Left are some badges my dad kept, a NE Marine Eng ARP Warden badge, John and Thomas Boundey name tags, and several Boys Brigade awards.

Bill used to love drawing and right, is one of the drawings he made for my mam, which he drew on his birthday in 1948 (date on the back of the drawing).

Before they could move into their first house together, my parents lived with my mother's grandparents in North Terrace, near St Peter's Church, Wallsend. The first home they had together was in Bewicke Street, Willington Quay by the Tyne Pedestrian Tunnel. Other homes have included Taunton Close, a maisonette in one of the 14 Storey flats; Windsor Drive, a ground floor flat in a three storey building in Howdon; and then Holderness Road, behind the Legion Club on Tynemouth Road, Howdon.

Below left is one of my dads' Motor Fuel Ration Books and below right is one of his units from the book which have been saved intact. How many people can remember these?

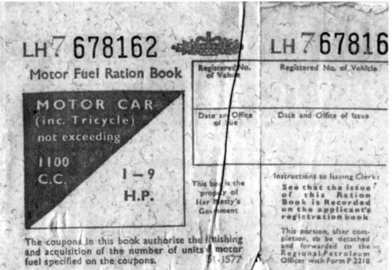

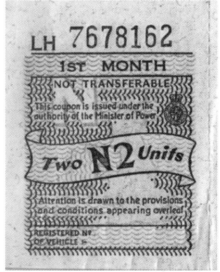

Two of my favourite photos of my dad. The far left shows him proudly showing off his RAF uniform and the nearest one shows him in his smart suit.

Gone But Not Forgotten

The Borough Theatre

The Borough Theatre stood on the corner of Station Road and Park Road. It was opened in 1909 and was built by the owner, Councillor Joseph Duffy, who was elected Mayor of Wallsend in November 1909 until he unfortunately died in July 1910 during his term of office. It has been the Gaumont Cinema, a theatre, a bingo hall and a dance studio and has been home to several shops which were incorporated into the building.

Sadly, in 2011, it was decided that nothing could be done to save the building and it was demolished to make way for a housing development. The first photograph shows the decoration on one of the boxes in the hall. The bottom photo shows the decor of the stairway before the theatre closed.

As a member of the Wallsend Local History Society, I was lucky enough to be able to get inside the Borough Theatre and take these photos before it was demolished. In an old issue of the Wallsend News, dated Friday, 3rd January 1953, the following article was published (although not shown in its entirety):

To the High Street ... to the Borough Theatre, that happy congenial place of stirring strains, red plush and perhaps dearest of all, the warm proximity of the performers when you actually and literally 'caught their very eye' as you applauded. Gone forever must be that dear intimacy, for in those days we moved in far smaller orbits and the population of Wallsend was naturally much smaller. It was just as if our seats were reserved, so regular were our movements.

Who among our older friends can forget the mad, grubby, glorious invasion upon the 'Gods' when early doors opened, or the annoying metal poles in The Pit?

Who cannot remember the heavy rattle of those monstrous brass rings that

carried the red plush curtains and the tiny head of James Appleby, who played the piccolo with all his verve and with every fibre of his being? And who does not recall those chorus girls who, on somewhat closer observation, always emerged with dusty knees and thighs after half-an-hour of horse-stepping and high-kicking?

I remember that outstanding revue called 'Buds and Blossoms', and how we all declared that the girls were most certainly 'blossoms' but stoutly contested their claims to be 'buds' for in our assertion many moons had passed since their 'budding'.

But we loved 'The Borough' and the artists too. I have special memories of 'Les Georges', father and son, who often sang 'You are my heart's delight'. George Moncreif was a fine tenor, a one-time plater. And well I recall him – short, rather stout, smart with a military grey moustache and greying hair parted down the middle. He left Swan's for the stage and how was I to know that years later I would have his yellow waistcoat and grey wig tenderly placed in my hands by a nephew of his with whom I was acquainted? 'Les Georges' were beloved by Old Wallsenders.

Many will remember Tommy Farmer who was in due turn both patron and performer at 'The Borough', who adopted the stage name of Tom E. Bradley. Tommy was a canny fellow, a good comedian and perhaps a rather indifferent 'slapdasher' on occasions at Wallsend Slipway.

That homely stage often knew the cream of the entertainment world in those days – George Robey, Harry Tate, Harry Nelson, Florrie Ford and a host of others. Their efforts were, as we know, un-aided by microphones and all the present-day supports and the fun was always clean and wholesome.

Our picture and music halls were an important part of our lives and we visited them all in turn. Strange it is that the present 'Queen's' in Station Road was once called 'Kings'. Time and time again it failed and went bankrupt, but once its name changed it began to flourish.

Old Wallsenders will remember the old chapel hall in North Road just past Greenland's fisheries, which was used as a cinema. 'The Royal', newly built, took its place, while the 'Tyne', our old favourite still packs them in. Happy it is to look back upon those less complicated days and lovely are those sacred associations

The photo above shows the snack bar of the theatre or bingo hall and the photo below was taken from the balcony doorway and overlooked the building which was once a social club and then later the Council Offices, which have also been demolished to make way for a new housing development.

of thoughts which can lay hold of our hearts and minds in these early hours of a New Year.

The Royal or 'Ranch'

The Royal cinema, or 'Ranch' as it was known due to the fact that it showed mainly western films, stood on High Street East, opposite the Brunswick Church. Today, Lloyds Bank is on the site of the former cinema. The Ranch was demolished in 1964.

Bigges Main Village

In 1923 Bigges Main had a population of only 690 people. The village was added to the old parish of Wallsend, which also included Willington High Row and Low Row, the farmstead of the Rising Sun Farm and the new Rising Sun Colliery, on 9th November 1910. The Hindmarsh family, who were largely interested in Wallsend and Willington, owned the lands in the 17th century. Elizabeth Hindmarsh married Thomas Bigge, son of Thomas Bigge, attorney-at-law of Newcastle, in 1705. Their son, William Bigge, who was born on 25th March 1707 and married Mary, daughter of Charles Clarke, succeeded to the estates on 29th January, 1736 and the land stayed in the Bigge family until 1862 when Matthew Robert Bigge sold the land to Mr David Burn.

Bigges Main Colliery commenced in July 1784. Three shafts were sunk and the miners' cottages were built, which became known as Bigges Main. The colliery was closed in 1857 when it was 'drowned out' by a flood which covered the mid-Tyne coal area. Wallsend council bought the land in 1961, to build a sports centre and this opened in 1970.

Swan's cranes

End of an era

All of the photographs on this page, apart from the one on the bottom left, were taken on 4th June 2010 when the cranes that have been used to build ships at Swan, Hunters & Wigham Richardson shipyards for many, many years were finally demolished. The first explosion was set off at 10.10 am. Exactly one minute later the dust had settled and the two cranes were no more.

St Aidan's Church

St Aidan's Church on Rosehill Bank was opened on 6th February 1907. The original door was situated in the square part of the church visible to the right of the cross. Later a new extension was built and the entrance door faced south, as in the photo on the right. The cross, which is a Memorial to the First World War was removed from its place in 2005 and situated in Holy Cross Cemetery on St Peter's Road before this church was demolished in August 2006.

Old steps to Holy Cross Church

The original steps leading to the Holy Cross church, here just visible to the right of the new steps, are now covered over by grass. They used to have platforms at certain intervals so that the pall-bearers carrying the coffins to the church could have a rest, as the hill was quite steep.

Strettle Memorials

This family business was situated at the southern end of the Burn Bridge and at the junction with Church Bank until vandalism forced Strettle's to move location.

My wife, Audrey, remembers an inscription on one of the stones reading something like:

'The kiss of the sun for pardon,
The song of the bird for mirth,
You're nearer to God in the garden,
Than anywhere else on earth.'

Howdon Library

The old Howdon library was opened in 1959 and was located on Churchill Street on the site of what used to be the original Wallsend Golf Club and later became part of land used by the Army during the Second World War. It became unfit for purpose during its later years and was opened part time before being demolished in 2009.

It was granted £1.3 million Lottery funding and has been turned into a state of the art Family Learning Centre which was officially opened by former TV news reader Mike Neville and the then Elected Mayor of North Tyneside, Linda Arkley on 30th January 2010. Mike Neville, MBE, is a local lad who was born in Willington Quay on 17th October 1936. He went to the Addison Potter Infant and Junior School and then the Stephenson Memorial Secondary Modern, as it was known when he attended, joining in 1947 and leaving in 1951, aged 15. He also officially opened the new Stephenson Memorial School on Martin Road on 16th July 1999.

Above are four photographs showing the inside of the original Howdon Library.

The photo right shows the new Howdon Library and was taken around the time it was first opened in January 2010.

George Angus Factory

The George Angus factory once stood on the north side of the Coast Road, opposite the 14 Storey flats, approximately where Wickes and B&Q are now.

Below are four photographs showing George Angus' apprentices being trained.

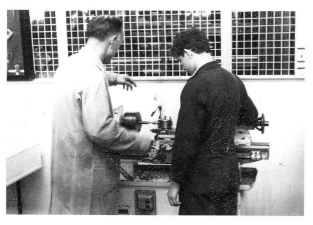

14 Storey Maisonettes

Although these were known as the 14 Storey flats, the Tenancy Agreement Rent Book had the words 'Block of Flats' crossed out and the name 'Maisonette' written in.

My parents moved into these maisonettes paying their first week's rent of £1.7.6d on 12th December 1960. They paid their last rent payment of £1.13.3d on 28th September 1963.

Part of their tenancy agreement terms were: 'Nothing must be thrown from the doors or windows' ... 'The tenant will not keep any animals in the tenement' ... 'The tenant will not use the tenement as a shop for the sale of goods' and 'No television aerial may be erected without prior approval ...'

The two photos on the left show the school, now the Langdale Centre, and the streets around the area of the 14 Storey flats, Mitford Gardens flats, Langdale Gardens, Melrose Gardens, Kendal Gardens and to the left of the school is the A19.

Interesting Times in Wallsend
Rawdon Court

Rawdon Court was a complex of flats located to the south of the Newcastle to Coast railway line and just north of Swan Hunter's Shipyard. The first of the following photos show Rawdon Court as seen from Wallsend Metro Station, looking west, supplied by Freda Davidson (now Graham). The others are of Rawdon Court being demolished and were supplied by Barry Martin.

The four photographs above show work underway on the construction of the slipway at the top of Station Road leading on to the Coast Road. Photos supplied by Michael Doolan.

The two photographs on the right show the A19 roundabout at the Coast Road junction under construction. Photos supplied by Denise Booth. They were taken from the top of the 14 Storey flats and are views looking east towards the A19, Formica Factory and Norham Road.

The following images were supplied by Freda Davidson and show different events which happened in Wallsend in the 1970s and '80s.

Wallsend March

The pictures below are from a march through Wallsend, either for the Miners' strike or a Trade Union march, which ended up at the Ritz Theatre on High Street West.

Wallsend Park

The pictures below show children playing on the climbing frames and swings in Wallsend Park, the Wallsend Bowling Pavilion and bowling green and a group of children and adults, thought to be from the Buddle Arts Centre setting up and playing on a giant bouncy platform.

Wallsend Shops

The following photos were taken in a shop in Wallsend Forum. They look as though they were taken in the Presto store which was at the entrance to what were the In-shops and was one of the shops where my mother, Elsie, once worked.

Rhythm Records

In 1989 my sister-in-law, Barbara Graham, took over the record shop on Station Road which was known as Tompkins. The shop was split into two halves, one selling records and the other selling bicycles. These photos show the shop as it was then and as I remember it – each wall full to the brim with records, posters and magazines.

In 2013 the shop was refurbished and developed as a coffee shop/sandwich shop. When the outside of the shop was decorated and the old shop sign taken down, the old Rhythm Record shop sign was still visible.

A silver disc presented to Rhythm Records to recognise 1,200,000 sales in the UK for the Whitney Houston song 'I will always love you'.

The newspaper article below from Friday, 3rd January 1958 describes a 'unique event where more than 50 veterans of the Boer War and the First World War' were to be entertained at the Drill Hall on Vine Street, Wallsend at a special Christmas and New Year party which was to be held on Saturday, 4th January 1958. The event was such a big occasion that an advert was placed in the same newspaper to inform any guest to the function that transportation to the party could be arranged with just a phone call. It is unknown if the phone number '63965' was for a taxi cab firm or for other arrangements to be made by the Council.

WALLSEND NEWS

TELEPHONE: WALLSEND 5-4114   High Street East, Wallsend.

No. 171   FRIDAY, JANUARY 3, 1958   Postage 2½d.   Threepence

Squadron has everything in readiness for a special Christmas and New

ORROW IS PARTY NIGHT
OLD BRIGADE'

Take your partners...

OFFICE BOY NOURS LIST
Two men Wallsend honoured

★

Special transport arranged: 'phone Wallsend 63965

A UNIQUE event in the history of Wallsend will take place tomorrow evening when more than 50 veterans of the Boer War and the 1914-18 war with their wives will be entertained in the Vine Street Drill Hall of the 506 Field Squadron Royal Engineers, TA to a Christmas and New Year party.

It was on October 25 that Wallsend News first published the story of the party which was to be held by the Squadron and immediately the response was over...

Who can remember the 'Market Woman' statue before it was moved to its present location?

Schools We Went To

Richardson Dees School

Here is a collection of class photos from the Richardson Dees School from different years. The first photo is a class from 1950 provided to the school by Angela Batey. Unfortunately there are no names provided.

The following two photographs are from the Richardson Dees School of March 1953 and show just some of the classes of that year. Again there are no pupils names provided.

Richardson Dees School, Class 7 in 1953. The Head Teacher at the time was Miss E. Nattrass.

Another photograph of the children of the Richardson Dees School dated March 1953. This photograph shows what is thought to have been a music class in the school hall.

In January 1987 the children of the Richardson Dees First School raised a sum of money which they donated to Dr Barnardo's charity. Here is the presentation of the cheque.

The Western School

Western Secondary Modern School, 1958-59. The only name provided with this photo is Tony Carr, middle row, second from the left – who provided the picture.

Above: A class from the Western Girls School of 1963-64.

Left: A Western School class from the mid 1960s. My wife, Audrey (née Graham) can be seen 5th from left in the front row.

The Central School

The Central School was located behind the Burnside School and overlooked the Burn and the Burn Bridge. It used to be split into two schools – a boys' and a girls'. The entrances to these can be seen in the two photos below.

When it first opened in 1913 it was a girls' secondary school and a boys' secondary school. In 1952 it became a mixed junior school and a mixed senior school.

It was then kept as a mixed junior-secondary school until 1969 when it was combined into a middle school – Central Middle School.

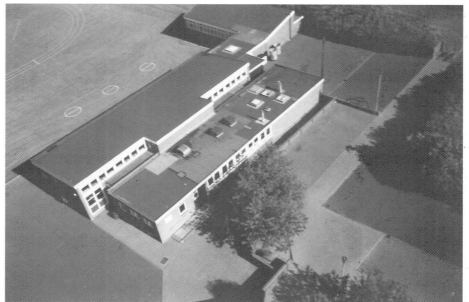

When the school was due to close teachers and pupils formed a group, called 'The Enterprise Group' and put together a booklet about the school's history – the following information is taken from that booklet:

Head teachers –

Boys' Secondary
Mr Forster – 1913-32
Mr J.W. Dawson – 1932-37
Mr J. Scorer – 1937-46
Mr J. Martin – 1946-52

Girls' Secondary
Miss E. Terry – 1913-26
Miss M. Kerr – 1926-50
Miss B. Dawson – 1950-52

Central Mixed Secondary School
Mr J. Martin – 1952-57
Miss D.A. Martin – 1957-66
Mr E.A. Snowden – 1966-69

Central Mixed Junior
Mr J.W. Watson – 1952-64
Mr F. Osselton – 1964-68

Central Middle School (Wallsend)
Mr E.A. Snowden – 1969-76
Mrs G.M. Keenaghan – 1976-85
Mr S. A. Hickson – 1985

There were two plaques mounted on the wall of one of the buildings.

The first plaque read –

'Wallsend Central Council Schools. Erected 1913'

and the second read as follows –

*'Sites and buildings committee.
Ald. G. Elliott, J.P. Mayor Chairman. Ald. J. O'Hanlon, J.P. Ald. R.H. Jackson. Coun. R. M. Anderson. Coun. T. Anderson J.P. Coun. J. Mullen. Coun J. Scorer.
Mr R. Wallis. Mr M.W. Graham Secretary'*

Central Secondary School Staff of 1968 included:

Miss Butler – Geography and PE.
Mrs Doris Wade – 3c class teacher, English.
Mrs O.P. Langley – 4m class teacher, English and History.
Mr E.A. Snowden – Headmaster from 1966.
Mrs M. Whealon – Needlework.
Mrs J. Trousdale – Part-time Remedial teacher.
Mr Noble – (known as 'Nobby') 3a class.
Mr B. Hindson – 2m class English, who was later to become head of fourth year.
when the school became a middle school.
Mr Weir – 1w class. Woodwork and Field Studies.
Mr Mcfarlane – Art and Pottery and was always called 'Mac'.
Mr Elgar Lumsden – 2l Music.
Mr R. Laverick – Deputy Head.
Mr Lemin – Science.
Mr Bruce – PE.

Right: The Covered Way. In 1969 when the Covered Way was built, a square piece of the playground was cut off from the rest – this area was called the 'Secret Garden'. There has been an argument that this extension was called the 'covered' or 'cupboard' way. Coat hangers were fastened to the wall giving it the look of a cupboard.

Below: Here are more views of the school.

The numbers in the photograph on the left were painted on to the playground in the Secret Garden. They are a version a game which was played throughout schools and was known as 'Hopscotch'. There were several layouts of the game but all basically had the same rules and as I remember, an empty shoe polish tin was used to play this game.

These photographs show the sad demise of this once proud school. Although I did not attend this school, I can still remember it, especially this view as it overlooked the Burn, a place where I used to play quite often when I was a young boy.

The photograph left shows the school class from 1947. Head master Fred Martin. Back row: ?, ?, David Kilpatrick, ?, ?, ?. Second back row: ?, ?, John Smily, ?, ?, ?, ?, ?. Middle row: Stewart, ?, ?, Robert Anderson, Peter Moor, Rom McOnicy, Harry McMillen. Second front row: Mick McLeary, White, ?, ?, ?, Jim Hepple, ?. Front row: ?, ?, ?, ?, ? McArther, ?, ? Apologies if any names are either wrong or mis-spelt.

The photo right shows a class from the Central School on a school trip to the beach and was supplied by Sandra Lammie (second from the right in the back row).

Central School Staff. Back row: Youldon, Varley, Clementson, Moore, Grundy. Middle row: Webster, Lawson, Blackburn, Carnatfan, Garland, Moore, Mills. Front row: Wilson, James, Atkin, Sykes, Keenaghan, Bowbeer, Oliver, Wilson, Anderson.

The Stephenson Memorial School

In an article in an old edition of the Newcastle Guardian dated Saturday 20th November 1858 was the following information:

Tuesday the 16th was observed as a day of general rejoicing and of great stirrings in the usually quiet village of Willington, the occasion being the laying of the foundation stone of the schools which are to perpetuate the memory of the late Mr George Stephenson. It was also the birthday of Mr Robert Stephenson.

The site of the new buildings, as our readers are probably aware, is one on which stood until recently the cottage in which Mr Robert Stephenson was born, and in which his parents resided for many years, the late Mr Stephenson being then employed as a brakesman to the ballast wharf.

The site contains a quarter of an acre of land, having a frontage to the river of one hundred feet, and was the gift of the Newcastle Corporation. The buildings will consist of school rooms for boys, girls and infants, with a house for a master and mistress attached, and a large library and reading-room for the use of the neighbourhood. The boy's school room will be 58ft x 20ft and will accommodate about 150 boys, and be arranged for a lecture room when required. It will be entered in the front by a richly carved stone doorway, surmounted by a panel in which will be a representation in stone of a locomotive engine, and underneath upon a scroll, the following inscription: *'Robert Stephenson, born Nov 16, 1803.'*

The infant school will be about 30ft x 18ft, and will accommodate upwards of 100 children. Over it will be the girls' school, of the same dimension, and lighted by a large traceried window which on the outside will combine a handsome niche to contain a statue of George Stephenson, and form one of the principle features in the front of the building. The roofs are to be formed of timber stained and varnished and over the centre of the boys' school is to be an octagonal bell turret, the sides being filled with traceried panels, the top covered with ornamental lead work, and supported in the inside upon four arched ribs resting in carved stone corbels. The buildings are designed in the Gothic Style and will have a highly ornamental and novel appearance on account of the introduction of a great deal of moulded work in red and blue bricks with stone dressings, a style of building which is new to the neighbourhood, and the merit of introducing which belongs to the architect.

The title of this picture is: 'The Stephenson Memorial School, Willington.' Foundation Stone Laid by Mrs Addison Potter, 16th Nov 1858. Archibald M. Dunn Esq, Architect. (Newcastle.) Supplement to the Daily Chronicle & Northern Counties Advertiser, 17th November 1858.

Another drawing of the school from, the other direction, showing part of the Lord Byron public house which was located next door to the school.

The contractors are Messrs Gibson and Stewart, the carpenters work being taken by Messrs Waite and Howard. The total cost will exceed £2,000. The plans have been approved by the Government, who assist the scheme by a grant. Mr Robert Stephenson has also, we understand contributed munificently to the funds.

On entering the village signs of bustle and rejoicing were everywhere visible, in banners and devices, whilst the cannon on the ballast hills were prepared to announce the event of the day. From the front of Mr Addison Potter's extensive brick and retort works were suspended large banners supporting an imposing device of the Newcastle Corporation Arms, which at night was illuminated with gas. In connection with the same works was another gas device displaying in prominent characters the letters 'G and RS'.

Mr Potter's works were the assembly ground for the company, who began to arrive about one o'clock. Among those present were the Right Worshipful the Mayor, Joseph Laycock, Esq, E. Potter, Esq, of Cramlington Hall, Mayor of Tynemouth, and Mrs Mayoress and Miss Potter, R. Pow, Esq, of Tynemouth, R.P. Philipson, Esq, of Newcastle, Thomas Sopwith Esq, of Allenheads, Mrs and Miss Sopwith, Mr and Mrs Addison Potter, Mrs Aubone Potter, Dr and Mrs DeMey, Mrs T.A. Cook, Wallsend, Mrs Ormeston, of Carville, Miss Robson, Mrs G.W. Armstrong, Mr and Mrs Charles Palmer of Whitley Hall, Mrs E.D. Thompson of South Shields, Mr D.R. Ramsay, of Jarrow, Mr Charles Weatherley, Howdon, Philip H. Stanton, Esq, Solicitor, Newcastle, G.W. Stable Esq, Solicitor, Newcastle, Dr J.C. Bruce, Rev. John Reed, Chirton House, W.H. Budden, Esq, Newcastle, Mr Moffatt, Surgeon, Howdon, Mr Henry Salkeld, Howdon, Mr W.A. Falconar, Howdon, Mr Robert Wallace, Newcastle and Mr Miller, Newcastle.

At two o'clock the company moved to Mr Potter's works to the site of the corner stone. The honour of laying the stone was entrusted to Mrs Addison Potter, and all things being in readiness, there was presented to the lady a silver trowel, which had been manufactured by Messrs. Lister and Sons, bearing the letters 'GS' and 'George Stephenson, born 9th June 1781.' On the other side the letters 'RS' surmounted by the words 'Robert Stephenson, born 16th Nov, 1803.' It also bears the following inscription:

'The foundation stone of the Stephenson Memorial Schools, at Willington Quay, was laid by Mrs Addison Potter, on the 16th Nov. 1858. A. M. Dunn, architect.'

In the bed of the foundation stone there was provided the usual cavity into which was placed a bottle containing coins and copies of local newspapers, together with a scroll containing a record of the event. A copy of the scroll we give below. These preliminaries having been attended to, Dr Bruce offered up the following prayer: 'Almighty and everlasting God, Thou has made all things, Thou sustaineth them, Thou has formed all things for Thine own glory. We pray that Thou wouldst smile upon this undertaking. O let this building be erected for thine honour, and here let multitudes of young people be trained up in the knowledge and in the righteousness filled to perform well their part in the world, and prepared for the world that is to come. Lord, we pray of Thee that Thou wouldst bless the honoured individual who was born on this spot and to whose honour this building is about to be reared. Give unto him renewed health and strength, and let all spiritual blessings in heavenly places in Christ Jesus be his, and when he falls, may it be as a shock of corn, full and ripe, and may those children trained up in this institution be enabled to follow in the footsteps of our honoured friend and of his honoured father, in so far as they may have been able to follow the perfect model, Christ Jesus. Oh Lord, we again entreat Thee that Thy blessing may crown the part about to be performed and that this building may be intended to the good of men and to the advancement of Thy Glory. Oh, May Thy Kingdom come throughout the world. May Thy will be done on Earth, as it is in Heaven, and Thine shall be all the glory. Hear us, and pardon us, for Christ's sake. Amen.'

The bed of the stone was then covered with mortar, in the laying on of which Mrs Potter assisted. The stone was lowered into its position, and the lady adjusted it with a mallet and plummet. She then amid protracted cheers, said: 'Ladies and Gentlemen, I hereby declare that the Foundation Stone of the Stephenson Memorial Schools is truly laid, and I call on you all to join with me in wishing every success to the undertaking. As in the elder Stephenson we see what talent unassisted by education can effect, so in the Son we learn that the two when combined become invincible, and I trust that under the blessing of God these schools will prove a benefit not only to this, but to succeeding generations.'

(Applause) The crowning work was a salute from the ballast hill battery.

The manuscript enclosed in the bottle was as follows:

THE FOUNDATION STONE OF THE STEPHENSON SCHOOLS
Was laid on the Sixteenth Day of November, One Thousand
Eight Hundred and Fifty Eight
By
MRS ADDISON POTTER

Trustees

George Robert Stephenson
Robert Stephenson, MP
Joseph Whitwell Pease
Addison Potter
William Weallens
Phillip Holmes Stanton

Archibald Matthias Dunn (Architect)

William Gibson and James Stewart (Builders)

The ground for these schools was presented by the Corporation of Newcastle upon Tyne. The building occupies the site of the Dwelling House formerly the Residence of George Stephenson, in which his son Robert Stephenson, was born, on 16th November, 1803. The funds for these schools were raised by Subscription, to which Robert Stephenson munificently contributed.

The Stephenson Memorial Middle School

The following extract is taken from a report of the opening ceremony of the school:

A new Stephenson Memorial School was opened on 2nd January 1932 on the site at Howdon Lane, to replace the old school building in Stephenson Street, Willington Quay.

The designer was Percy I. Browne and Son, architects, Newcastle, and the general contractors were Messrs A.V. Clercy and Sons, of Sunderland. The cost of the building being £38,594.

The school was an imposing design but adopted for practical use accommodating 480 boys and 480 girls. It was planned around two courts and there were nine ordinary classrooms accommodating 40 pupils each, one special subject room, a library, and in a technical and handicrafts building there were four handicraft rooms and two art rooms. Special attention was paid to the lighting arrangements for the admittance of sunlight. Each quadrangle was occupied by a garden and the central portion was arranged to permit open-air teaching in the sheltered surroundings. In each portion of the school there was a large hall with a stage. The centre of the eastern front was occupied by the staff rooms.

A meal room and drying room were also provided. The playgrounds were constructed of concrete and there was a running track of a distance of approximately 125 yards on the straight.

The famous fireplace (*right*) in the meals room, together with the model of the cottage over it, in which Robert Stephenson was born, were removed from the old school to the new school and in the centre of the front there was a fine replacement representation of the famous 'ROCKET' engine.

The opening ceremony was performed by Councillor John Mason, Chairman of the Wallsend Education Committee. The Mayor, Alderman W. North, presided the event.

On behalf of the architects and the builder, Councillor Mason was presented with a silver tea service. Councillor Mason gave an address in which he referred to educational work in the borough.

A vote of thanks was proposed by Alderman J. Mullen and seconded by Alderman J. Timlin. The company afterwards inspected the schools and were entertained to tea. Mr J.G. Jewells, formerly headmaster at the old school, will be head of the boys' department and Miss F. Cook, who had been transferred from the Bewicke School, will be headmistress.

The photograph left shows some of the seniors at work in one of the classrooms.

Below are the mantelpiece, which was once in the Stephenson Memorial School, showing the initials 'RS' for Robert Stephenson, and the model of the Stephenson's cottage which used to stand in Stephenson Street, Willington Quay.

I have been asked by many ex-pupils of the school 'Do you remember the model and whatever happened to it?'

It is believed that the model is now located at the Stephenson Railway Museum in Middle Engine Lane.

The photograph above shows the Stephenson School playing field. In my school days the football pitch ran from east to west in the foreground of the photo. The canteen is the light coloured building on the right. The building in the centre was the caretaker's house. The building on the left with the pointed roof was the science laboratory.

A class from Stephenson Boys' School that was taken in the school hall, names and dates not supplied. The photo was supplied by Joan Paxton.

A young girl's school memories

I commenced school in 1939 at the Bewicke Infants, which was situated on Tynemouth Road. It is no longer there having been demolished some years ago and the site is now a Health Centre.

As the Second World War commenced that year, our school was taken over by the ARP (Air-Raid Wardens). Their job was to distribute gas masks to everyone in case the Germans used deadly gas, which fortunately, they did not. We were all transferred to Stephenson Memorial School which had to accommodate infants, juniors and senior pupils.

Air-Raid shelters were built down the right hand side of the playground, which shut in the light from the classrooms, making them very dark. When a warning siren was given all pupils had to file into the shelters. We would sing songs and recite poetry and try not to be too frightened. If you wanted to go to the toilet whilst in the shelters you had to go outside the door and use buckets. You were not allowed to leave the shelter until the all-clear had sounded, or you may have been killed.

We had assembly every morning, said our prayers and sang hymns for half an hour. We were taught science, maths, English, geography, history, art, domestic science, needlework and PE. Although we had very little equipment for PE – I think a netball and posts and shintey stick and goal nets were all we had.

A Miss Cooke was the Headmistress then and there was only one married teacher, a Mrs Hutchinson, who took us for needlework, the rest were all single women.

When you went into the senior class you were given teams, e.g. Austin, Bronte, Cavelle and Darling, the teams all named after famous women. Each team had a colour, Austin was red, Bronte was green, Cavelle was yellow and Darling was blue. I chose to be in Cavelle team and you remained with that team until you left school. There was great rivalry between the teams, as you got a shield at the end of term for the best. Cavelle always seemed to win and I was very proud.

At Christmas time we would hold a concert in the school hall. Anyone with a good voice or who could recite would get up on the stage and do their stuff. We once did a play 'Alice in Wonderland' and I got the part of the Dormouse.

Even though conditions were very bad due to the war, food was rationed and school dinners were always the same, corned beef, potatoes and plenty of cabbage, we did get milk every morning and afternoon. Sometimes the Education Authority would visit the school and measure your feet and if you had no shoes they would provide laced up boots, which were hated, but are very fashionable today.

Teachers had a very difficult time, but gave us a marvellous education. I must add that the discipline was very high and the belt was used often if you misbehaved or were late three times in a week. I was once given ten belts, five on each hand, for having ten spelling mistakes out of twenty given. We took it all as a matter of course and it did not do us any harm.

by Patricia Glasspool (Glasspool was the maiden name of my paternal grandmother but it is not known if this was one of her relatives although it is very possible.)

The staff from the 1970s with just a few names supplied: Back row includes: Mr Colin Boyle, Mr David Dobinson, Mr Knowles and Mr Raymond Taylor. In the centre of the front row is Mrs Bruce, Headmistress.

The photograph left was supplied by Mr Colin Boyle, the teacher standing in the centre of the back row. The date of the photograph is unknown and the only person I can recognise is Robert Keddy in the front row on the left.

Addison Potter School

The photograph above shows the class of the Addison Potter School in Willington Quay and the date given is from the 1950s. Judging by the cards on the wall, it looks like the photo was taken around the Christmas time, with a young Sheila Hamil (née Appleby) on the right side of the see-saw.

Addison Potter Schools, Willington Quay. 3755

A wonderful old picture postcard of boys outside Addison Potter Schools from around 1920. The postcard was sent to Leadgate, County Durham with this message on the back: 'Hope you are going strong as we are very canny.'

The Jubilee Infants' School

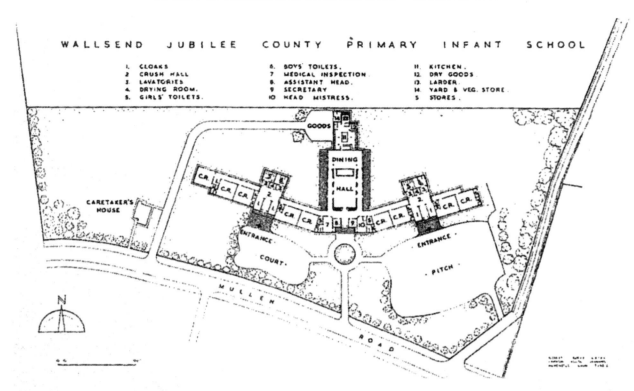

The plan above and the following information come from the brochure of 'The Official Opening of the Wallsend Jubilee County Primary Infant School' when the school was opened on Thursday, 30th September 1952 at 2.30 pm.

The school was designed by Robert Burke, the Quantity Surveyor was R.H. Duns and the Building Contractor was H.E. Pitt Ltd. The estimated cost of the building was £67,000 and the furnishings cost £6,700.

The programme of events were as follows:

After the guests assembled in the hall the Opening Prayer was performed by the Mayor's Chaplin. The Introduction of the Proceedings was read by the Mayor of Wallsend, Alderman A. Sutherland JP and this was followed by the Official Opening and Naming of the school by Alderman Mrs A.M. Hyde (Chairman of the Education Committee). The Dedicatory Hymn, The Pilgrim's Hymn, was next and this was followed by the Presentation of the Bouquet before the school performed 'Rhythms and Mimes'.

Next came the Handing Over of the School by Councillor Mrs E.W. Mitchell (Vice-Chairman of the Northumberland County Education Committee).

Mr R.W. Burke then performed a Presentation on behalf of the Architect, Surveyor and Contractors, which was followed by a Vote of Thanks by Alderman P.J. McArdle JP (Vice-Chairman of the Education Committee).

The proceedings were completed by the singing of the National Anthem before light refreshments were served in the School Dining Hall before the School was open for inspection.

When the Jubilee School opened in 1952 the staff consisted of:

Miss M. McBain – Headmistress,
Mrs M.E. McKinnon,
Miss A. Bowman,
Miss M. Robson,

Miss M. Temple,
Miss E. Read,
Miss M. Harwood,
Mrs G.E. Carruthers.

Right: The staff of the Jubilee School in the restroom.

Below: This photograph is taken from the Jubilee Primary Infants School album dated February 1953.

Jubilee Infants Primary School class 4, 1953. Back row: ?, ?, ?, Bobby Hamil, ?, ?, ?, Mildred Dent, ?, ?, ?, ?, Alan Ogle. Middle row: Melvyn Askew, ?, ?, Doreen Fraser, Jeffrey Bowmer, Raymond Glindon, ?, Harry Wedderburn, Waveney Scott, Ian Weatherburn, Christine Rickleton. Front row: Selwyn Grey, Joan ?, Audrey ?, ?, Anne Rickleton, Valerie ?, ?, ?, ?, ?, ?. Most of the names for the photograph have been supplied by Bob Hamil, back row fourth from the left.

Left: Miss Margaret McBain, Headmistress of the Jubilee School for 19 years, posing for her retirement after nearly 40 years as a teacher with several of her pupils. Born in Sunderland, she was also treasurer of the local branch of the National Association of Head Teachers.

Above and below: Two classes from the Jubilee School in 1953.

Jubilee Infants Primary School Dinner Ladies in the school canteen in 1953.

By 1969 the school had grown and consisted of the following staff:

Mrs M. McBain, Headmistress, Mrs H. Pinkerton, Deputy Head, Miss M. Harwood, Mr W. Stoker, Mrs M. Landles, Mrs C. Carr, Mrs B. Watt, Mrs J. Robinson, Miss D.S. Thompson, Miss J.M. Prickett?, left in December 1969, Miss S.M. Wilson, Mrs E. Smith, part-time and Mrs A. Bolton who commenced in 1970.

The Buddle Infant School

A report by the Ministry of Education HM Inspectors on the Buddle County Primary School (Infants Dept) dated 25th June 1951 states that it was well known that it was overcrowded but that the pupils would soon be moving to a new school. The Headmistress, Miss M. McBain, had done a great job and was kept on as Headmistress of the new school – the Jubilee School.

Buddle School Class 3A – 1957. Back row: Ian Phillipson, ?, Maurice Benn, Ronnie Martin, ?, ?, ?, Ray Glindon, ?, Melvyn Askew, ?. Second back row: ?, Bob Hamil, ?, ?, Alan Benn, Louie Bradeford, Alan Fatkin, Dave Eland, ?, ?, Malcolm Bramley, Billy McNaughton. Second front row: ?, ?, Ian Weatherburn, ?, ?, ?, Alan Ogle, ?, Alan Turner ?, ?. Front row: Godfrey Banks, Eric Edwards, ?, ?, ?, ?, ?, ?, Harry Wedderburn, ?

The Wallsend County Technical School, (Burnside School)

The photograph on the right shows the Wallsend County Technical School class of T1, dated around 1960 – unfortunately, it is slightly blurred.

Most of the names have been supplied. Starting at the back left: Ken Snowdon, John Gibson, Michael Hogarth, John Robinson, Barry Wilkinson, Bob Hamil, Dorothy Gill, Christina Rickelton, Ann Harrington, Julie Barr and Kathleen Costello. Second row: Philip Watson, Keith Davison, Telford Irving, Ian Lowe (deceased), Kevin Conway (deceased), Brenda Thompson, Barbara Ward, Georgina Garnic, Mary Thompson and Linda Gill. Third row: Rob Philip and Keith Saville. Sitting (nicely): Alan Fletcher, Margaret Richardson and Margaret Claringbull. The photograph was taken by Dave Moore in 1961, a Physics teacher fondly recalled. It was supplied by Neil Salkeld along with the following story:

The photograph was taken from within the new Boyd Road building, shortly after the formal school opening. All but two pupils have been identified in this classroom scene, where they all seemed only too happy to stop work and have their picture taken!

It all seems a long time ago – and yet seems like yesterday. Looking back, schools in the late 1950s and early '60s seem so very different from those nowadays. I think we all knew life was changing for young people as the 1960s marched on. But we hardly had time to stop, think and watch as those weeks, months and years just flew by and, as reminded frequently, GCE exams beckoned. For many children, GCEs were the route to employment at aged 16; not that many went on to University.

The decades of starting, experiencing and leaving work also flew by and time has sadly claimed two very well-known and popular school colleagues shown in this picture. Ian Lowe died in 2009 and his visits to Whitley Bay kept us in touch after meeting again a few years earlier. Ian had not lost his dry sense of humour and, if anything (and somehow), his Yorkshire accent had somehow become even more apparent since school. Ian was one of the exceptions at school in qualifying for University. Well qualified in IT, his last job had been as a Consultant at Hewlett Packard in Reading. Kevin Conway died shortly after Ian and was similarly very well-liked and respected. Disabled through polio in his early years, Kevin wore a leg brace as some children did in those days. Looking back, Kevin's personality, determination and example in all he did was an inspiration to us all.

The County Technical School was officially opened at 2 pm on 15th July 1960.

The Order of Ceremony was as follows:

– The proceedings will open with a Service of Dedication.
– Alderman the Rev. R.E. Robson, Chairman of the Education Committee, will introduce H.H. Mullens, Esq, BSc, MIEE, Chairman of C.A. Parsons & Co Ltd, and of A. Reyrolle & Co. Ltd.
– Mr Mullens will give an address and declare the school open.
– His Worship the Mayor of Wallsend, Councillor W. Rickleton, will propose and Councillor H.W. Clark, will second a vote of thanks to Mr Mullens.
– National Anthem.
At the end of the Ceremony the school will be open to inspection.
Headmaster – G.B. Austin, BA, BSc

Wallsend County Secondary Technical School was a four-form entry school, admitting approximately 120 children each year at the age of eleven-plus and providing for them a complete five-year course up to the age of sixteen and sixth form courses after that for those who desire them. The school, situated in the centre of the Borough of Wallsend on Boyd Road, was planned to accommodate 660 boys and girls and comprised of a large hall with a well-equipped stage for dramatic production, gymnasium, library, 12 classrooms and 4 division rooms, music room and social studies room and on a practical side, 2 housecraft and 1 needlework room, commerce room, art room, craft room, 4 science laboratories, drawing office, machine shop, metalwork shop, 2 woodwork shops, supplemented by a full provision of kitchen and dining facilities, staff room, medical inspection room, cloakroom and sanitary accommodation.

Building work began on the 8th July 1957, and the first pupils, after a temporary sojourn of some twelve months in the Hadrian Secondary Modern School, were housed in their own premises for the first time on the 5th January 1960. The total cost of the building work including professional fees was just over £252,000. In addition furniture and equipment cost about £27,000.

The school was designed by and erected under the supervision of Mr C.C. Brown, ARIBA, County Architect, in collaboration with Geo. H. Gray and Partners, Chartered Architects and Surveyors, 52 Camden Street, North Shields.

The Consulting Engineers for the structural work were Messrs. L.G. Mouchel & Partners Limited, of Newcastle; for the heating, electrical and water installations, Messrs. Cairns & Byles, Newcastle.

The Quantity Surveyors were Messrs. J.W. Summers & Partners, Newcastle. The General Contractors were Messrs Hastie D. Burton Ltd, King Street, North Shields. The Clerks Of Works were Mr R. Arkle and Mr J. Campbell. The layout of the grounds and preparation of playing fields were carried out under the supervision of the Education Committee's Schools Grounds Officer.

The Willington Middle School

A class from Willington Middle School, around 1970. Back row: Unknown, Robert Easten, David Bowie, Paul Fiddler, Richard Irving, Michael Cairns. Middle row: Paul Scott, Martin Blair, Jeffrey Pickard, Jimmy Walsh, Michael Brydon, Tony Patterson, Raymond Dalglish, Anthony Webster. Front row: Brenda Adams, Lesley Hills, Patricia Rowntree, Marjorie Spinks, Denise Booth, Lynda Fender, Lesley Wilson, Marjorie Cowley?, Susan Watkin, Yvonne McGuinness, Linda Abbott.

A class from Willington Middle School, around 1970s. Back row: Martin Blair, Raymond Dalglish, Christopher Jackson, Robin Spink, Steven Thompson, Gary Hutchinson, Paul Scott. Middle row: Anthony Webster, Ian Cotcher, Ian Scott, Susan Lake, Shirley Weatherall, Marjorie Spink, Paul Fiddler, David Bowie, Brian Curry, Mrs Tonks. Front row: Marilyn Miller, Nicola Cowen, Lynda Abbott, Janette McKenzie, Jill Raynor, Denise Booth, Audrey Graham (now my wife), Sharon Horne, Michelle Beaton (my cousin).

Groups

Wallsend Technical School's version of 'Toad of Toad Hall' which was held at the County Technical School on Thursday, 16th March, 1961. The cast included: Sheila Weddell, Carrol Shannon, Anne Lynch, Eleanor Fenwick, C. Hogg, A. Park, D. Cruddace, H. Lambert, E. Limbrick, D. Platt, K. Moore, A. Henderson, M. Laverick, J. Bell, R. Varley, A. Harper and A. Patterson. Also taking part were the pupils of Form IY who were the chorus of weasels, ferrets, stoats and 'voices off'.

Wallsend Technical School play from around 1962. Back row: Ann Lynch played Carolyn, Pauline Farries was Bula, and Malcolm Laverick was Arthur with Alan Park in the white coat. Front row: Sandra Lane played 'Ma' with Hughie Price as 'Pa'. This was an American play in which Hughie drove an imaginary car with other pupils as passengers. As you

do in such a play, they all sat on chairs in such a way so as to replicate a driving scene. The author was a famous American playwright, possibly Tennessee Williams.

Many of you might remember Alan Park as the man who used to fix the watches in the old Co-op store in Wallsend Forum. Hughie Price is the manager of Tynemouth Lodge public house.

Pupils from Wallsend County Technical School at Ford Castle in 1962. Starting from the bottom of the photograph. Front row: Ford Castle Tutors, Keith Saville, Linda Gill, Brenda Thompson, Anne Wright, Jennifer Heslop, Philip Watson, Mrs Benson*. Second row: Ian Ellis, Neil Salkeld, Pauline Farries, Ann Harrington, Kathleen Costello, Ken Snowdon. Third row: Margaret Lumsden, Ann Douglas, Waveney Scott, Jennifer Mews, Janis Ainsley, Pamela Quinn. Fourth row: Janice Tindle, Keith Davison, Barry Wilkinson, Sandra Pomeroy, Alan Fletcher, Valerie Howes. Fifth row: Ian Lowe, Kathleen Hastie, Margaret Richardson, David Watson, Christine Bunn, Alan Park. Back row: Michael Hogarth, Bob Hamil, John Robinson, Raymond Anderson, Ed Cork, Richard Varley. * Mrs Benson (if memory serves correctly), a Wallsend Tech Geography teacher with joint Field Trip stewardship alongside photographer, fellow Tech Geography teacher and Monkseaton Morrisman Alan Brown. Sadly Mr Brown died, a few years after our school leaving, in the late 1960s.

One of the pupils in the photo above, Philip K. Watson, remembers his time at Ford Castle:

It was a beautiful early June morning and we Tech 'Coast Pupils' were collected early from the old Whitley Bay Bus Station. Mr Alan Brown (Geography Teacher and of Monkseaton Morrismen fame) made his presence felt and we were allocated seats – boy next to girl – no doubt so we would behave! It made you feel quite grown up, not necessarily sitting next to a girl but going away for the week without your parents. We then picked up the rest of our school friends along the route, including those at Boyd Road, Wallsend.

The journey was impressive as was the final destination. Ford Castle in North Northumberland with its magnificent grounds is a spectacular sight. This was absolute luxury! But neither the time nor the place to be homesick though! Sharing a room was never a problem – except these were your school friends!

This was a Field Geography Trip and we were soon reminded of the reason for being there – part of GCE O level Geography! The main focus was to look at the formation of the land and to determine the reason for the village's location.

It's difficult to recall the various walks and smaller assignments with certain colleagues. One can recall a farm visit with Richard Varley and one or two others – collecting material for a project on return. It was very warm, tiring but wonderful at our age. We were shown rivers (including Ox Bow lakes) and Ingram and College valleys and one can recall seeing a crashed RAF plane still fairly intact as we climbed yet another hill after Cheviot Hill. Drinking from a stream was allowed only after water testing by Mr Brown. Once, some of the pupils slept in a turret – how cool was that!

Outside there was a croquet lawn where we tried to play the game – in a way it was all quite Harry Potterish!

Socially, one can recall the Thursday night was dance night. They had been playing the B. Bumble and the Stingers Nutrocker music for about an hour – time after time. Then – last minute – no dance and no reason!

All great experiences though with good people – and you would hope that young people have had the chance of such experiences since then.

I am extremely grateful to principally Neil Salkeld and Kathleen Costello for providing these wonderful memories of a very rare visit to unknown pastures away from home without the care and attention of our parents!

A drama group at Ford Castle. There are two Wallsend Technical pupils included in what is an excellent photograph showing many drama students.

Often used by schools in the 1960s, Ford Castle was of exceptional quality, very well situated in North Northumberland and enjoyed by many schoolchildren at that time. From personal memory (other than drama!), the experience there made you feel quite grown up!

Away from normal school and above all, away from your loving parents for a while it was an escape from routine! Whilst no more than two Tech pupils can be identified, many more people on Tyneside and in Northumberland may well be able to identify themselves and others in what is an exceptional picture.

The date is estimated as being summer 1962. The two Tech pupils are Paul Simnet – third row from the front, second from the left and Hughie Price – fourth row from the front, extreme right. One play performed was entitled 'Murder in the Old Red Barn' in which Hughie played the lead role. In the 1960s, there is no doubt that to stay at Ford Castle was luxury in the extreme, an absolute privilege and an experience never forgotten. (Thanks to Hughie Price and Neil Salkeld.)

Ford Castle where thousands of children from Tyneside and Northumberland spent many happy days.

Some of the miners' wives from the Rising Sun Cottages about to go on a bus trip. Not all of the names could be supplied and the names that have been supplied come with the husband's names in brackets – the date is unknown. Mrs Esther Coulson (Bobby), Mrs Harriet Hamil (Jack), Mrs Jenny Banks (non-miner), Mrs Geary (Chucks), Mrs Stephenson, Mrs Williamson (Albert) and Mrs Rynn (Jimmy).

A Willington High School class of 1977 reunion, held at the Engine Inn in 1993 including: Audrey Graham (with the cheeky wave and smile), Susan Lake, Kerry ?, Pauline Myers, Leslie Hill, Michelle Beaton, Janette McKenzie, Dorothy Thompson, Gail Johnson, Susan Moat, Sonia Robson, Jean Rycroft, Kim Thompson, Veronica Cranmer, Andrea Willmott, Sharon Horne and Jackie Willmott.

Mayoress Joyce Rickleton at the Northumberland leek, vegetable and flower show which was held between 22nd and 25th September 1960. Included are: Mayoress Rickleton, Mr I. Smith, Councillor J.C. Grogan and Barney Wood.

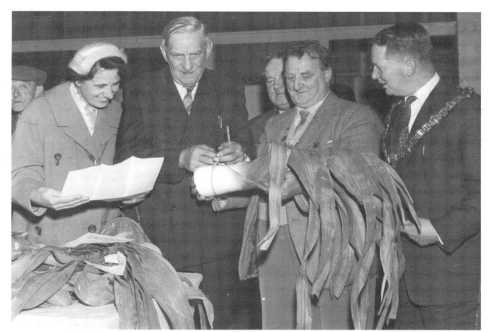

Mr Bloomfield offering a lucky dip to guests at the Mayoress of Wallsend Charity Ball which was held at the Wallsend Memorial Hall in 1960. (This photograph and the one above were supplied by Christine Rickleton.)

This photograph, thought to be of the Mayor's Procession through Wallsend, shows Mayor Elsie Halliburton with Town Clerk John Stoker to her right, about to lead the procession. Others in the line-up are: Councillor Mollie Brown, 5th from left, Sir Neville Trotter (MP for Tynemouth for many years) behind the Town Clerk, Alderman Sowerby behind the Mayor and Elsie Booth.

The photograph right is of the Bigges Main Carnival of either 1970 or 1971. It shows members of the Low Willington Farm Revellers, LWR, who were dressed in a royal blue and silver uniform and Howdon Hussars, (HH), who were dressed in a green and black uniform. Left to right: HH Drum Major, HH Bass Drummer, LWR Band Major – Maureen Grey, LWR Mascot, Mayor of Wallsend

– Councillor Elsie Halliburton, HH Mascot, LWR Bass Drummer – George Young, Mayoress of Wallsend – Elsie Booth, LWR Drum Major – Lorraine Iddon and HH Band Major.

Low Willington Revellers – photo taken around the early 70s in Pembroke Gardens. Included are: Majorettes Linda Cartright and Jackie Iddon, Bass Drummer Elaine Pomphrey. Drummers: Coleen Pearce, Lynn Beadling, Pat McKeown, Roz Chambers. Others include: Gwen McIntosh, Cath Chambers, Sally-Ann Gustaveson, Rosie Goodin, Enid Potts, Lilian Gibson, Margaret Owen, Denise Booth. (Apologies if any names are mis-spelt). Photos and as many names as possible supplied by Denise Booth.

Above: Celebrating the Queen's Silver Jubilee at a street party in Monmouth Gardens, Howdon, on 7th June 1977. Left to right: Margaret Stephenson, Barbara Graham, Hazel Ellis, Jackie Gosling, Margaret Chambers, Susan Richardson, Sheila Graham and Mary Graham. (Photo supplied by Bella Graham).

Right: A certificate awarded to Audrey Graham who attended the Monmouth Gardens Silver Jubilee Street Party.

1952-1977

BE IT KNOWN THAT

Audrey Graham
being a Loyal Subject
of
Her Majesty Queen Elizabeth the Second
did attend the
MONMOUTH ST PARTY
on 7TH June, 1977
to commemorate the Silver Jubilee of
our Gracious Majesty

1977

Left: More celebrating – this time a Coronation Party in Glover's Row for King George VI in 1937. Left to right: Teene Young, Meg Preston, Mrs Kerr, Alice Straker, Mrs McKeown, Annie Reay, Granny Timlin, Mrs Hudson, Mrs Dodds, Mrs Carter, Mrs Straker, Granny Grimes and Mrs Tierney or Tierny.

The Wallsend and District Choral Society

In the 50th Anniversary programme for the Wallsend and District Choral Society the following was written by the founder member of the Society, Ken Warren:

In the latter part of the 1940s, the Allen Memorial Methodist Church, Wallsend, engaged a new Caretaker/ Choir Master, one David (Dave) Fuller. Under his leadership the church choir carried out their usual duties, leading the singing of hymns and performing an anthem each Sunday evening. On special occasions such as Easter singing a cantata 'Olivet to Calvary' or 'The Crucifiction.'

The choir was about 30 plus strong and well balanced, and Dave felt that it could tackle greater things and suggested that they could perform concert versions of Opera. The choir recoiled somewhat at this, but were persuaded that they could do it!

The first work they performed was 'Maritana' by William Wallace. This was given for a week in the Church Hall, and proved to be a great success, and had whetted the appetite of the choir for more.

Next came Gounod's 'Faust' and the choir invited members of Hadrian Road Methodist Church Choir – the daughter church of 'Allen' – and the choir of St Luke's Church to come and join them.

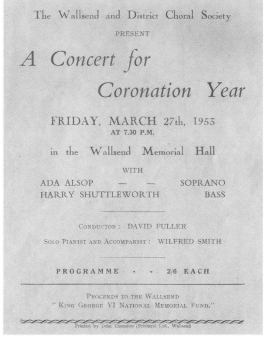

Above: A programme for 'A Concert for Coronation Year' on Friday, 27th March 1953, held at the Wallsend Memorial Hall.

During this performance which was given for a week, an innovation was introduced. During the last act the organ in the church was linked up by speakers within the hall so that a glorious conclusion to the opera was achieved and at the same time a cross was illuminated behind the choir.

'Tales of Hoffmann' by Offenbach was the next venture, which was given for a week and was another success.

During this time the accompanists were Norman Coates, the Church organist, Wilf Smith, and Ken Varty. Ken being responsible for the link up of the organ in 'Faust'.

The soloists who sang with the choir during this period were Elly Short, a Greek Soprano, Dan Minay, Bass, a friend of Dave Fuller, who came each year on a week's holiday from the Isle of Man, Stan Davies, tenor, Tom Hall, tenor, Ralph Ridley, tenor and Fred Lawson, tenor.

By this time so many members had joined that it was no longer the Allen Memorial Church Choir and thus it was agreed in 1951 that the choir be called the Wallsend and District Choral Society, with an annual subscription of 5 shillings (25p)!

WALLSEND AND DISTRICT CHORAL SOCIETY

5oth Anniversary Concert

Saturday 18th May 2002

at CIVIC HALL WALLSEND

Left: The Society celebrated their 50th Anniversary with a concert held at the Civic Hall in Wallsend on Saturday, 18th May 2002.

The Wallsend Wesleyan Sunday School trip to Ryton from before the First World War. Ryton Willows was a popular destination for day trippers for many years – in particular for Sunday Schools.

Left: Father Scriven with the staff of St Aidan's School, Willington Quay around 1932. Father Thomas Scriven (who was a Clergyman at St Aidan's Church between 1930-46), became a hero of the bombing of Headlam and Hodgson Streets during the Second World War on the night of 25th April 1941. Featured in 'Wallsend Remembered', page 17.

Right: Staff of the Pearl Cinema on its opening day – Monday, 21st November 1910. The proprietors were the Pearl Picture Palace Ltd and the General Manager, presumably the gentleman in the centre with the top hat, Edward Wilcock.

Sport

Above: Burnside Community High School under-15s Netball Squad, 1991. Back row: Julie Chambers, Carla Arrowsmith, Rachel Morley, Sarah Hamil. Front row: Lianne ?, ?, Fiona Levin, Kelly Powell, Kerry Williams.

St Aidan's School Senior Netball Team of 1962. Photograph supplied with permission of St Aidan's Church.

Wallsend Netball Team, 1970. Back row: Susan ?, Val Levin, Sheila Hamil, Jean Dotchin. Front row: Jen Ruscoe, Marge Davidson, Katie ?

Wallsend Lawn Tennis Club

Members of the Wallsend Lawn Tennis Club pose for this photograph. Back row: George Carson, George Robinson, Phil Burke, auditor, Jim Priestley, Austin Blaylock.
Second back row: Jimmy Greenhill, with baby, Mrs Greenhill, Harry Levin, Ann Featonby, Lillian Humble, John Henderson, ?. Second front row: Audrey Gannen, Brenda Humble, ?, ?, ?
Front row (seated): Nancy Levin, Mrs Lorrains, Frank Levin, Irene Levin, Jenny Hickleton, Joan Robinson.

Wallsend Lawn Tennis Club late 1950s/early '60s. Left to right: Frank Levin, ?, ?, ?, ?, Jim Priestley, Ann Featonby, John Foster, ?, Sam Bagnall, ?, Susan Brew, Alan Gallagher, Peter Marshall, Harry Levin, Brian Corners, George Swaddle, John Sullivan, ?

Another photograph of Wallsend Lawn Tennis Club, around 1939 and the only names supplied with this photo are back row: Frank Levin (2nd from left), Harry Levin (4th from left) and Jenny Hickleton (7th from left). Front row (kneeling): Lillian Humble (2nd from left) and Irene Levin (7th from left).

In an old edition of the Wallsend News, 18th July 1958, there was the following article:

Harry Levin – Wallsend's Mr Badminton and Lawn Tennis
The future of Wallsend Park Tennis Club is resting in the hands of a few farsighted people who are taking the trouble to coach youngsters on the finer points of the game. One of the originators of this training scheme is Mr Harry Levin, who is this week's sporting personality. Forty-seven year old Mr Levin, of The Crescent, Wallsend is one of the veterans of the club. Since he joined the club in 1933 he has held every position – president, secretary, captain of the men's team, treasurer and match secretary. He has been a regular team member since joining the club when they played in the Tynemouth Mixed Doubles League and partnered Elsie Yellowley and Edith Jowsey. In 1935 they won both divisions of the league.

When the club transferred to the Tyneside Works League in 1939, he partnered Jenny Hickleton as a mixed doubles partner and for the men's team, Austin Blaylock, who still plays for the club. Although the club also won both divisions of this league, the trophy was never presented to them due to the intervention of the war.

A highlight of Mr Levin's career was in 1935 when in the final of the Tynemouth League Men's Doubles knock-out competition and partnering the club's all-round champion, George Hilton, they defeated A. Hilton and W. Milburn of Windermere Club. The match lasted two hours and 40 minutes, and after losing the first two sets, 8-10, 1-6, they took the next three 7-5, 9-7 and 6-3.

Like most sportsmen, Mr Levin interests himself in other games. His keen interest in badminton led him in 1946 to found the Wallsend and District Badminton League, of which he is still secretary and treasurer, and is also secretary of St Luke's Badminton Club.

Mr Levin, who is laboratory manager at the Rising Sun Colliery and also scientific representative on the executive committee of the British Association of Colliery Management, played football in his youth in the Newcastle Churches League and acted as their secretary.

'That was in the days when the boys had to strip anywhere they could and carry the goalposts to the ground,' said Mr Levin, who is also deputy vicar's warden, sidesman and member of the St Luke's Church Council.

Then in the summer with the same group of lads he used to play friendly cricket matches on the Burn Closes.

Neil Levin, Harry Levin's son, has kept most of his father's Tennis and Badminton documents and has now donated the collection to the Wallsend Local History Society. It is a fascinating collection of old season cards, scorecards, photographs and newspaper cuttings that will be saved and categorised for display at our meetings for the members to read.

Right: A ticket for the Badminton League Annual Dance and a Match Scoring Book from the 1940s.

Below: Wallsend Park Tennis Club letterhead.

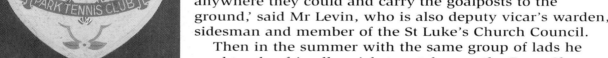

WALLSEND BADMINTON LEAGUE

ANNUAL DANCE
to be held in the
LINDISFARNE CLUB,
WEST STREET, WALLSEND
Tuesday, 22nd April, 1969
Licensed Bar   -   7-30 - 12

TICKET   -   -   -   4/6

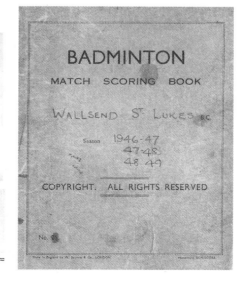

BADMINTON
MATCH SCORING BOOK
WALLSEND ST. LUKES B.C.
Season 1946-47
47-48
48-49

COPYRIGHT. ALL RIGHTS RESERVED

WALLSEND PARK TENNIS CLUB

Secretary:	President:	Match Secretary:
T. A. Blaylock,	C. Hickleton, Esq.	A. H. Levin,
101 Park Road,		141 High View N.
Wallsend		Wallsend 63244

Committee Duty Nights

Monday	Colin Jackson
	Harry Levin
Tuesday	Sheila Armstrong
	Evelyn Appleby
Wednesday	Rose Cassie
	Ron Gray
Thursday	Alma Graveling
	Ralph Busby
Friday	Peggy Harle
	Frank Levin

Saturday Tournament

Members intending to enter must have names on sheet **before 2-15 p.m.**

All day tournaments will be held on June 2nd, July 7th, August 4th and September 1st. Players entering are expected to stay till the finish.

Shepherd Bros., 22, North Terrace, Wallsend.

Wallsend Park Tennis Club

SEASON 1951

Northumberland & Durham

Inter-Club Tennis League.

FIXTURES.

DATE		OPPONENTS		F.	A.
		Gentlemen's Team Group G.			
Tues.	May 22	Reyrolles II	A	3	3
Wed.	May 30	Boldon II	H	9	0
Mon.	June 4	N.E.E.R.C.	A	5	4
Sun.	June 10	Linden Grove II	A	9	0
Wed.	July 11	Swan Hunters	H	2	4
Mon.	July 16	Sunderland III	A	5	4
		Ladies' Team Group L.F.			
Tues.	May 22	Houghton	H	8	0
Tues.	May 29	Hawthorn Leslie	A	7	2
Tues.	June 5	Boldon II	A	3	6
Fri.	June 8	Eslington I	A	3	6
Tues.	July 3	South North'ld II	H	7	2
Tues.	July 10	Grainger II	A	6	3

Officials

Ladies' Captain	Lilian Humble
Gent's Captain	Frank Levin
Secretary	Austin Blaylock
Match Secretary	Harry Levin
Treasurer	Kath Baker

Committee

Colin Jackson	Harry Levin
Sheila Armstrong	Evelyn Appleby
Rose Cassie	Ron Gray
Alma Graveling	Ralph Busby
Peggy Harle	Frank Levin

Selection Committee

| Ladies' : | L. Humble, E. Appleby, K. Baker. |
| Gent's : | F. Levin, C. Jackson, A. Blaylock. |

The inside and outside of the Wallsend Park Tennis Club, season 1951 booklet shows Committee members, Officials and dates and results of matches in that year.

The Wallsend Badminton League Presentation which was thought to be held at the old NESCO club at the top of Kings Road. The only names supplied are left to right: ?, ?, ?, ?, Frank Levin, Alice McAndrew, ?, Pat Maher, Tom Dalziel, ?, Harry Levin.

The North Tyneside Sports Town, 1977 third round winners of the Badminton League, with only a few names supplied. Back row: Pat Cowan (2nd left) and Bruce Cherry (1st from right). Front row: Harry Levin, ?, Yvonne Hoyland, ? Alan Young, ?, ?, Christine Forsythe.

Wallsend Rugby Football Club

by Ed Jackson, Past President

The earliest reference we have in our archives is a typewritten A5 sheet referring to 'the 1st AGM of Wallsend RFC at the Coach and Horses on 10th May 1881'.

Then a copy of 'Borough of Tynemouth Rugby Club' fixture list of 1882 records their 3rd XV game at Wallsend 2nd XV, which Tynemouth won by a goal (converted try) and 7 tries to nil. Early Wallsend fixture lists in our possession are: 1889-90 which includes games against Percy Park II's, Rockcliffe II's and Tynedale II's.

1890-91: Opponents include Consett, Gosforth, Percy Park and Tynedale firsts. We also won the County No 3 competition.

1897-98: Matches versus Percy Park Firsts, Carlisle, Westoe, West Hartlepool, Tynedale, Durham City, Rockcliffe and Northern (who we beat 45-0 at home and 18-0 away!). It was around this time that Wallsend were at their peak, providing three players, including the Captain, of the Northumberland County side which won the RU County Championship in 1898. In 1899 and 1900 Wallsend won the County No 2 competition.

The next fixture list in hand is 1933-34, including: Ashington, Consett, Tynedale, Swan's (relevant later), Blaydon, Westoe and North Durham, although at what level isn't evident.

The Club seems to have led a 'gypsy' existence in the 1920s and '30s. We have conflicting records by now-deceased 'Old Boys'. From 1926-29 our home was the Boundary Ground, this being the terminal point of the tram service from Newcastle. In the early 1930s we were at either Stott's Farm (adjoining Swan Hunter's Recreation Ground) or Sanderson's Farm at Daisy

Walllsend Rugby Union Football Club, November 1979.

Hill. Mid to late 1930s found us at Dene Park, Battle Hill (which may have been Bowran's Farm).

During the Second World War all our fixtures were played away at local Armed Services bases. The war brought the loss of seven players killed in action.

A great revival took place after 1945 due to the generosity of Farmer Day and his sons Peter and Tom. Day's Farm at Willington Square was the home ground for a further nine seasons until old members hung up their boots and interest was lost locally. One of our correspondents from those days states that from 1954 to 1959 Wallsend combined with Swan Hunters under the name of 'Wallsend', but this is doubtful as we have a copy of a card originally headed 'Wallsend RFC' but annotated & altered to 'Swan Hunters RFC' – this is dated 1954 and signed by Alf Yeoman – known to be a stalwart of Swan Hunter's Club. The connection with Swan Hunters was carried on until recent times of course, but we have records from the Company's magazine 'The Shipyard' with references to matches against Wallsend in 1935, 1937 & 1938, when Swan's teams were still 'cutting their teeth'.

The Wallsend Club of today came about due to the Swan Hunter Recreation Ground being given up during the great amalgamation of Swan's, Vicker's, Hawthorn Leslie's and Readhead's into 'British Shipbuilders'. Fortunately, the Sports Centre at Bigges Maine had been opened and we were invited to move 'lock, stock & goalposts' providing we changed our name to 'Wallsend RFC' and our colours to green and gold. So we left behind 'the Hut' and the communal concrete bath for our new home in 1969.

The metamorphosis from 'Swan's in blue' to 'Eagles in green' was not easy. We'd been our own masters with virtually no outside interference, but at the Sports Centre we were just another section and difficulties arose with regard to changing room availability and pitch condition control; plus the fact that we no longer had income from the bar but now had fees and charges imposed upon us which we hadn't been used to.

With regards to playing, those were the days before leagues were formed and all fixtures apart from cup competitions were arranged on a 'friendly' basis. We found that, despite our asking the 'senior' clubs in the County for 1st XV games, most would only deign to grant us 2nd or even 3rd team fixtures. Wallsend had few friends at our own level! However, perseverance eventually led to our winning the Northumberland Junior Shield in 1975, beating the much-vaunted Gosforth Falcons by 17 points to 13 at the old County Ground. Playing in that match were present-day stalwarts Jim Wrightson, Doug Pearson and Brian Thirlaway, who produced the longest drop-goal in the Club's memory – from the halfway line and a mere couple of yards from touch!

In 1983 Wallsend won the County Junior Cup (No 3 Competition). That team, 'Lowery's Men', included Jim Wrightson, Stu Robinson, Alan Flockton and the Robison brothers Gavin & Stu. Also in 1983, our long-serving County Representative Dennis Douglas was appointed President of Northumberland Rugby Union, an honour not previously attained by any Wallsend member.

Wallsend Rugby Union Football Club, 1983 Cup Winners. Back row: Steph Thirlaway, Marty Smith, Ed Smith, John Parkin, Sid Mitcheson, Mel Smith, Rob Muirhead, Chris Blackett, Stu Robinson, Colin Kemp and Gavin Robison. Front row: Alan Flockton, Stu Robison, Jim Wrightson, Rob Lowery, Daryl Smith, Steve Patterson and Don Sansom.

By 1991 life at the Sports Centre had become untenable and we moved over the hedge to Benfield School, where the 'clubhouse' was Sam Smith's Pavilion, under the auspices of Benfield Residents' Association. The move brought about an almost immediate success in our 3rd Team, Wallsend Eagles, being victorious in the final of the County Junior Plate Competition.

With the advent of Leagues in 1992, we began at last to prove our worth on the field in an officially recognised way. We knew that eventually we would find our true level and that previously reluctant senior clubs would be forced to honour the fixtures in the correct division.

Our efforts eventually came to fruition with our winning the County Senior Plate in 2007 against Gosforth and promotion as Champions of Durham & Northumberland Division 2. We held our own in the first season at the higher level, culminating in beating Northern at McCracken Park for the first time since 1897-98.

Many thanks to Gavin Robison for this information.

Wallsend Technical School under 15s – Back row: Dave Robertson (Metalwork Teacher), Geoff Athey, ?, Rob Phillips, Pete Preston, Barry Wilkinson, Mickey Hogarth, Den Hall. Front row: Brian Hill, ?, Brian Curran, Ted Limerick, Alan Fletcher, Ray Waller.

Hadrian County Secondary School football team, 1964. Front row: D. Clark, W. McClean, I. Crane, B. Taylor, D. Chaffey, A. Reynolds. Back row: T. Todd, E. Morris, R. Fallon (captain), R. Simpson, B. Chambers, M. Margeson, G. Skinner, K. Richardson and A. Docherty.

Father Scriven, right, with St Aidan's School Football Team of 1931-32. St Aidan's had a number of good football teams in the years before and after the Second World War and won the Wallsend's Schools League Shield on several occasions.

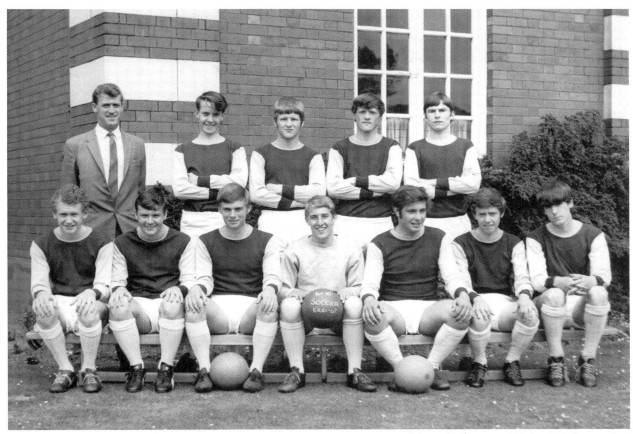

Wallsend Grammar School. Back row: Malcolm Berry (PE Teacher), John Cicconi, Martin ?, ?, ?. Front row: ?, Keith Dalby, Barry Garbutt, Eddie Tait, Steven Chater, ?, ?.

Carville School football team from 1964. Sitting on the far left is former Newcastle United player Albert Stubbins. The brilliant forward played for Newcastle just after the Second World War before signing for Liverpool and became an England international.

As a boy before the war,

Albert had played for the Carville School team. He remembered his time at the school in the magazine *Northern Football* in the 1960s: 'In the pre-war days, Carville played at Burns Closes, Wallsend, where it was possible for spectators to view more than one game at a time … In the 1930s we played in red and black striped jerseys, and black shorts, and like most schoolboys, we developed a strong liking for our particular colours. In those days, in order to ensure that the team was always well turned out, 'Scent' cards were sold to parents, relatives and friends.'

Wallsend Local History Society

The Wallsend Local History Society was formed in November 1973, holding its preliminary meeting at 7.30 pm on Saturday, 29th September 1973, at Battle Hill Community Centre, Wallsend.

The Organiser, Mr Ian Brown opened the proceedings and according to the notes, the people in attendance were President – Ian Brown, Chairman – R.J. Graham, with other members including Mr J. Robinson, Mr R. Graham (Secretary), Mrs M. Wallace, Mr J. Wallace, Mr Harrison, Mr Wylie and Mrs Wylie. Subjects which were discussed at this meeting, after Mr Brown expressed his pleasure at meeting all those present, were the possibility of restoring the old ruined Roman stones at Carville Chapel, Holy Cross Church Steps and the old village pump at the foot of Crow Bank.

Co-organiser Mr Robert Graham brought up the subject of future meetings and those present clearly indicated, by a show of hands, that they desired the next meeting to be held, if possible, in the Wallsend Central Library. The vote was 12 for, 3 absent and 0 against. The date of the next meeting was fixed at Saturday, 20th October 1973. At the close of the meeting at 9.25 pm, Mr Brown collected £1.60p for the funds.

The next meeting did take place on 20th October 1973 but for some unknown reason were held, not at the Wallsend Central Library, but at the St John Ambulance Head Quarters (the Church Hall) in Warwick Road, adjoining the United Reform Church.

The first Annual General Meeting took place on Saturday, 8th December 1973 at the Vine Street Community Centre, Wallsend. Elections – Mr Ian Brown was generally acknowledged to be President. It was agreed that Mr R. Graham to continue as Chairman and his wife be Secretary and for the duration, Treasurer. Nominations for the post of Vice-Chairman included – Coun. J. Cousins, Councillor K.S. Wylie and Mr J.H. Domonley. Mr Domonley was duly elected as Vice-Chairman.

The notes are hand written and are slightly difficult to read so hopefully the information is correct.

The Wallsend Local History Society Committee. Left to right: George Laws, Liz Liddle, Steve Boundey, Alan Maddison, Barry Martin, Phyllis Laws, Edmund Hall, Dorothy Hall, Ken Hutchinson, Elaine Borthwick, Lenny Fisher and Brian Robson.

Today the History Society is still going strong, celebrating 40 years in November 2013. We remember and are very grateful to past members and are proud to say that we now have more members than ever in our society. Our meetings are held on the second Monday of each month, from 7 pm to 9 pm and the attendance at our meetings always astound us. We would like to take this opportunity to thank all of our members, committee members and wide range of speakers for helping the society go from strength to strength.

Acknowledgements

Many thanks go to Neil Salkeld, Bob and Sheila Hamil and their school friends, Chris Rickleton, Hugh Price, Neil Levin, Freda Davidson, Michael Doolan, cousins Michelle and Dorothy, Margaret McGregor, James Bridgewood, Julie Frater, Denise Booth, Barry Martin, Tony Carr, George Nairn, Wallsend Local History Society, Ken Hutchinson and Don and Margaret Price. For the information on the Jubilee School, my thanks to Headmistress Mrs Ann Thornton and School Business Manager Nicki Willis.

A special thank you to Andrew Clark for having faith in me again.

Historical sources – 'The History of the Parish of Wallsend' by William Richardson, 'Images of Wallsend' and 'Wallsend Through Time' both by Ken Hutchinson, the Wallsend News, North Tyneside Libraries.

The document above is an Empire Day Certificate from 1915 which was awarded to Dorothy Winder, my maternal grandmother, who married Hugh Lammie, a Scottish lad who came to Wallsend from the Isle of Skye to look for work.

Back Cover:
The top photograph on the back page shows one of the PTE double decker buses on Station Road, heading towards Swan Hunter's and probably making its way back to the bus depot, which used to be located on Hadrian Road. The photo was taken before the tower of Segedunum Roman Fort and Museum and the Job Centre and shops (the Carpet Store and Asda, which was once Aldi) were built.

The bottom photograph shows an lady walking outside the St Columba's Church, with the High Street West shops by the Forum entrance in the background.

Both photographs were provided by Freda Davidson.

Also available from Summerhill Books

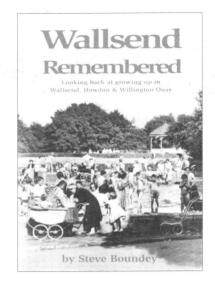

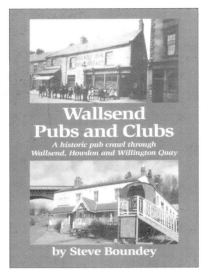

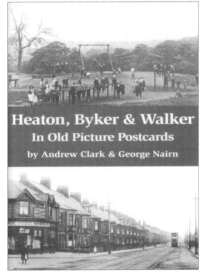

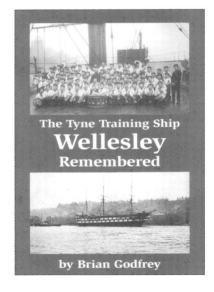

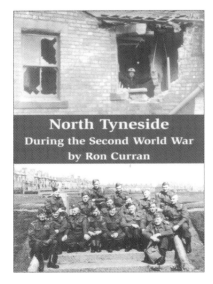

www.summerhillbooks.co.uk